THE WAY OF FAITH

THE WAY OF FAITH

Martin Luther

Compiled by
JUDITH COUCHMAN
and LISA MARZANO

SERVANT PUBLICATIONS
ANN ARBOR, MICHIGAN

Vine Books is an imprint of Servant Publications especially designed to serve evangelical Christians.

Scripture verses marked NIV are taken from the HOLY BIBLE, NEW INTERNATIONAL VERSION, © 1973, 1978, 1984 by International Bible Society. Used by permission of Zondervan Publishing House. All rights reserved. Verses marked NRSV are taken from the New Revised Standard Version Bible, © 1989, by the Division of Christian Education of the National Council of the Churches of Christ in the USA. Used by permission.

Compiled by Judith Couchman and Lisa Marzano.

Published by Servant Publications
P.O. Box 8617
Ann Arbor, Michigan 48107

Cover design: Alan Furst, Minneapolis, Minnesota

99 00 01 02 10 9 8 7 6 5 4 3 2 1

Printed in the United States of America
ISBN 1-56955-115-4

LIBRARY OF CONGRESS CATALOGING-IN-PUBLICATION DATA

Luther, Martin, 1483-1546.
    The way of faith / Martin Luther; compiled by Judith Couchman and Lisa Marzano.
        p. cm. — (Life messages of great Christians)
    ISBN 1-56955-115-4 (alk. paper)
        1. Spiritual life—Christianity Prayer-books and devotions—English.
2. Devotional calendars. I. Couchman, Judith, 1953-
II. Marzano, Lisa. III. Title. IV. Series.
BV4811.L88 1999   99-37123
242—dc21   CIP

In memory of Margaret,
a dear friend to the Couchman family.

CONTENTS

ACKNOWLEDGMENTS

Many thanks to the team at Servant Publications for supporting this book and the *Life Messages of Great Christians* series, especially Bert Ghezzi, vice-president of editorial. I'm also grateful to editor Liz Heaney and copy editor Deena Davis for their contributions to this book, and to Lisa Marzano, who helped with a significant share of the editing and writing.

And once again I thank those who prayed for me and the compilation process: Charette Barta, Opal Couchman, Win Couchman, Madalene Harris, Karen Hilt, Shirley Honeywell, and Nancy Lemons.

I n the face of adversity, it takes courage to stand up for what you believe. But thankfully for us, in the sixteenth century Martin Luther stood firm.

During a time of corruption in the church, Luther left the priesthood and began preaching that God's forgiveness was free, received through confession and faith. "Forgiveness of sins is not something which we can earn for ourselves by our own good deeds," he claimed. "Rather, it is a free gift which God gives to us as a result of all that Jesus did for us as our Savior. Salvation, therefore, is completely and only by faith in Jesus."

It was a revolutionary message, defying the Catholic church's sale of indulgences for the forgiveness of sins. It also returned believers to a simple faith in God's Word.

After opposing the pope's practices and nailing his objections to the door of the Castle Church in Wittenberg, Germany, Luther became outlawed in his own country. Still, the determined Luther believed that faith would make a way. He hid for a year, translating the New Testament into German so his countrymen could read it for themselves. When it was safe to emerge, Luther taught, preached, wrote hymns, and continued translating the Bible for the last twenty years of his life.

Luther's acts of faith ushered in the spiritual Reformation and birthed the Protestant church. His teaching spiritually transformed Europe and the world, leaving behind an unshakable legacy. His *Catechism,* the basic teachings of the Bible, have been used by churches for over four hundred years.

Luther married a former nun, Catherine von Bora, and they had six children. At sixty-three years old, he died, confident of his faithfulness to God. On his deathbed he prayed, "You, God of all consolation, I thank you for revealing to me your dear Son, Jesus Christ, in whom I believe, whom I have preached and confessed, whom I have loved and praised."

In this forty-day devotional drawn from Luther's sermons and writings, we're inspired to believe God's Word, live in righteousness, pray by petition, and obey the commandments. But most of all, to walk in the way of faith.

—*Judith Couchman,*
June 1999

PART ONE

Believing by Faith

Thy love and grace alone avail
To blot out my transgression;
The best and holiest deeds must fail
To break sin's dread oppression.
Before thee none can boasting stand,
But all must fear thy strict demand
And live alone by mercy.

Though great our sins and sore our woes,
His grace much more aboundeth;
His helping love no limit knows,
Our utmost need it soundeth.
Our shepherd good and true is he,
Who will at last his Israel free
From all their sin and sorrow.

From "From Depths of Woe I Cry to Thee"
by Martin Luther

MARTIN LUTHER'S INSIGHT
By faith we accept God's free grace and unlimited forgiveness.

DAY 1

The Surety of God's Word

God's Word will never fail or fade away.

WISDOM FROM SCRIPTURE

Your word, O Lord, is eternal; it stands firm in the heavens.

Your faithfulness continues through all generations; you established the earth, and it endures.

Your laws endure to this day, for all things serve you.

If your law had not been my delight, I would have perished in my affliction.

I will never forget your precepts, for by them you have preserved my life.

Save me, for I am yours; I have sought out your precepts.

The wicked are waiting to destroy me, but I will ponder your statutes.

To all perfection I see a limit; but your commands are boundless.

Oh, how I love your law! I meditate on it all day long.

Your commands make me wiser than my enemies, for they are ever with me.

I have more insight than all my teachers, for I meditate on your statutes.

PSALM 119:89-99, NIV

INSIGHTS FROM MARTIN LUTHER

That the Bible is God's Word and book I prove thus: All things that have been and are in the world, and the manner of their being, are described in the first book of Moses on the creation. Even as God made and shaped the world, so does it stand to this day.

Infinite potentates have raged against this book and sought to destroy and uproot it—King Alexander the Great, the princes of Egypt and of Babylon, the monarchs of Persia, of Greece and of Rome, the emperors Julius and Augustus—but they did not prevail. They are all gone and vanished, while the book remains, and will remain for ever and ever, perfect and entire, as it was declared at first.

Who has thus helped it? Who has thus protected it against such mighty forces? No one, surely, but God himself, who is the master of all things. And it is no small miracle how God has so long preserved and protected this book; for the devil and the world are sore foes to it. I believe that the devil has destroyed many good books of the church, as he has killed and crushed many holy persons, the memory of whom has now passed away, but the Bible remains.

The Holy Scriptures are full of divine gifts and virtues. The books of the heathen teach nothing of faith, hope, or charity; they present no idea of these things. They contemplate only the present, and that which man, with the use of his material reason, can grasp and comprehend. Look not therein for hope or trust in God. But see how the Psalms and the Book of Job speak of faith, hope, resignation, and prayer. The Holy Scripture is the highest and best of books, abounding in comfort under all afflictions and trials. It teaches us to see, to feel, to grasp, and to comprehend faith, hope, and charity, far more than mere human reason can. And when evil oppresses us, it teaches how these virtues throw light upon the darkness, and how, after this poor miserable existence of ours on earth, there is another and an eternal life.

We ought not to criticize, explain, or judge the Scriptures by our mere reason, but diligently, with prayer, meditate on them, and seek their meaning. The devil and temptations also afford us occasion to learn and understand the Scriptures, by experience and practice. Without these we should never understand them, however diligently we read and listened to them. The Holy Spirit must be our only master and tutor. When I find myself assailed by temptation, I immediately lay hold of some text of the Bible, which Jesus extends to me.

Oh! How great and glorious a thing it is to have before one the Word of God! With the Word we may at all times feel joyous and secure; we need never be in want of consolation, for we see before us, in all its brightness, the pure and right way. He who loses sight of the Word of God falls into despair. The voice of heaven no longer sustains him. He follows only the disorderly tendency of his heart and of world vanity, which lead him on to his destruction.

God alone, through his Word, instructs the heart so that it may come to the serious knowledge of how wicked it is and corrupt and hostile to God. Afterwards God brings man to the knowledge of God, and how he may be freed from sin, and how, after this miserable world, he may obtain life everlasting.

Human reason, with all its wisdom, can only instruct people about how to live honestly and decently in the world, how to keep house, build—things learned from philosophy and heathenish books. But how should they learn to know God and his dear Son, Christ Jesus, and to be saved? This the Holy Spirit alone teaches through God's Word, for philosophy does not understand divine matters.

I don't say that men may not teach and learn philosophy. I approve thereof, as long as it is within reason and moderation. Let philosophy remain within her bounds, as God has appointed, and let us make use of her as of a character in a comedy, but not mix her up with divinity. Nor is it tolerable to make faith an accident or quality, happening by chance, for such words are merely philosophical—used in schools and in temporal affairs, which human sense and reason may comprehend. But faith is a thing in the heart, having its being and substance by itself, given of God as his proper work, not a corporal thing that may be seen, felt, or touched.

—*Of God's Word*

QUESTIONS TO CONSIDER

1. How can you know that God's Word provides the absolute truth?
2. How can you study God's Word to hide it in your heart?

A PRAYERFUL RESPONSE

Lord, increase my love for and understanding of your Word. Amen.

DAY 2

God's Works Among Us

THOUGHT FOR TODAY

God's works are powerful and mysterious.

WISDOM FROM SCRIPTURE

How many are your works, O Lord! In wisdom you made them all; the earth is full of your creatures.

There is the sea, vast and spacious, teeming with creatures beyond number— living things both large and small.

There the ships go to and fro, and the leviathan, which you formed to frolic there.

These all look to you to give them their food at the proper time.

When you give it to them, they gather it up; when you open your hand, they are satisfied with good things.

When you hide your face, they are terrified; when you take away their breath, they die and return to the dust.

When you send your Spirit, they are created, and you renew the face of the earth.

May the glory of the Lord endure forever; may the Lord rejoice in his works—he who looks at the earth, and it trembles, who touches the mountains, and they smoke.

I will sing to the Lord all my life; I will sing praise to my God as long as I live.

PSALM 104:24-33, NIV

All the works of God are unsearchable and unspeakable; no human sense can find them out. Faith only takes hold of them without human power or aid. No mortal can comprehend God in his majesty, and therefore did he come before us in the simplest manner and was made man, sin, death, and weakness.

In all things, in the least creatures, and their members, God's almighty power and wonderful works clearly shine. For what man, however powerful, wise, or holy, can make out of one fig, a fig tree or another fig? Or, out of one cherry stone, a cherry, or a cherry tree? Or what man can know how God creates and preserves all things, and makes them grow?

Neither can we conceive how the eye sees, or how intelligible words are spoken plainly, when only the tongue moves and stirs in the mouth—all of which are natural things, daily seen and acted. How then should we be able to comprehend or understand the secret counsels of God's majesty, or search them out with our human sense, reason, or understanding? Should we then admire our own wisdom? I admit myself a fool, and yield myself captive.

When God contemplates some great work, he begins it by the hand of some poor, weak, human creature, to whom he afterwards gives aid, so that the enemies who seek to obstruct it are overcome. As when he delivered the children of Israel out of the long, wearisome, and heavy captivity in Egypt, and led them into the land of promise, he called Moses, to whom he afterwards gave his brother Aaron as an assistant. And though Pharaoh at first set himself hard against them, and plagued the people worse than before, yet he was forced in the end to let Israel go. And when he hunted after them with all his host, the

Lord drowned Pharaoh with all his power in the Red Sea, and so delivered his people.

Again, in the time of Eli the priest, when matters stood very evil in Israel—the Philistines pressing hard upon them and taking away the Ark of God into their land, and when Eli, in great sorrow of heart, fell backwards from his chair and broke his neck, and it seemed as if Israel were utterly undone—God raised up Samuel the prophet, and through him restored Israel, and the Philistines were overthrown.

Afterwards, when Saul was sore pressed by the Philistines, so that for anguish of heart he despaired and thrust himself through, three of his sons and many people dying with him, every man thought that now there was an end of Israel. But shortly after, when David was chosen king over all Israel, then came the golden time. For David, the chosen of God, not only saved Israel out of the enemies' hands, but also forced to obedience all kings and people that set themselves against him. He helped the kingdom up again in such manner that in his and Solomon's time it was in full flourish, power, and glory.

Even so, when Judah was carried captive to Babylon, then God selected the prophets Ezekiel, Haggai, and Zechariah, who comforted men in their distress and captivity, making promise not only of their return into the land of Judah, but also that Christ should come in his due time.

Hence we may see that God never forsakes his people, nor even the wicked, who by reason of their sins are severely punished and plagued.

God also deals strangely with his saints, contrary to all human wisdom and understanding. To that end that those who fear God and are good Christians may learn to depend on invisible things, and through death may be made alive again, for God's Word is a light that shines in a dark place. Esau was cursed, yet it went well with him. He was lord in the land, and priest in the church. But Jacob had to fly, and dwell in poverty, in another country.

God deals with godly Christians much as with the ungodly, yea, and sometimes far worse. He deals with them even as a house-father with a son and a servant; he whips and beats the son much more and oftener than the servant. Yet, nevertheless, he gathers for the son a treasure to inherit, while a stubborn and a disobedient servant he beats not with the rod, but thrusts out of doors, and gives him nothing of the inheritance.

God is a good and gracious Lord, but according to the first commandment, he proclaims, "Thou shalt have no other gods but me." He desires nothing of us: no taxes, subsidies, money, or goods. He only requires that he may be our God and Father. Therefore he bestows upon us, richly, with an overflowing cup, all manner of spiritual and temporal gifts, but we look not so much as once towards him, nor will have him to be our God.

[Yet] God is not an angry God. If he were so, we are all utterly lost and undone. God does not willingly strike mankind, except, as a just God, he be constrained to do so. But having no pleasure in unrighteousness and ungodliness, he must therefore allow the punishment to go on.

He that can humble himself earnestly before God in Christ has already won. God will have mercy on the poor and sorrowful, and spare them that humble themselves before him. Were it not so, no human creature would come unto him, or call upon him; no man would be heard, no man saved, nor thank him: "For in hell no man praiseth thee," says the psalm. The devil can frighten, murder, and steal, but God revives and comforts.

—Of God's Works

QUESTIONS TO CONSIDER

1. What has God accomplished in your life?
2. When do you most see God at work?

A PRAYERFUL RESPONSE

Lord, thank you that your ways are above anything I can imagine. Amen.

DAY 3

Who Is Jesus Christ?

THOUGHT FOR TODAY

We seek God through Jesus Christ, his Son.

WISDOM FROM SCRIPTURE

In the beginning was the Word, and the Word was with God, and the Word was God.

He was with God in the beginning.

Through him all things were made; without him nothing was made that has been made.

In him was life, and that life was the light of men.

The light shines in the darkness, but the darkness has not understood it.

There came a man who was sent from God; his name was John.

He came as a witness to testify concerning that light, so that through him all men might believe.

He himself was not the light; he came only as a witness to the light.

The true light that gives light to every man was coming into the world.

He was in the world, and though the world was made through him, the world did not recognize him.

He came to that which was his own, but his own did not receive him.

Yet to all who received him, to those who believed in his

name, he gave the right to become children of God—children born not of natural descent, nor of human decision or a husband's will, but born of God.

The Word became flesh and made his dwelling among us. We have seen his glory, the glory of the One and Only, who came from the Father, full of grace and truth.

JOHN 1:1-14, NIV

INSIGHTS FROM MARTIN LUTHER

The apostle Peter says: "Grow up in the knowledge of Jesus Christ," of that compassionate Lord and Master, whom all should learn to know only out of the Scriptures. He says: "Search the Scriptures, for they do testify of me." John says: "In the beginning was the Word, and the Word was with God, and the Word was God." Thomas also calls Christ, God, where he says: "My Lord and my God." In like manner Paul speaks of Christ, that he is God. He says: "Who is God over all, blessed forever, Amen." And, "In Christ dwelleth all the fullness of the Godhead bodily."

Christ must needs be the true God, seeing he fulfilled and overcame the law. For most certain it is that no one else could have vanquished the law, angel or human creature, but Christ only, so that it cannot hurt those that believe in him. Therefore, most certainly he is the Son of God, and natural God. Now, if we comprehend Christ in this manner, as the Holy Scripture displays him before us, then certain it is that we can neither err nor be put to confusion; and may then easily judge what is right to be held of all manner of divine qualities, religions, and worship that are used and practiced in the universal world.

Were this picturing of Christ removed out of our sight or darkened in us, there would follow utter disorder. For human and natural religion, wisdom, and understanding cannot judge truly the laws of God, which have exhausted and still exhaust the art of all philosophers—all the learned and worldly-wise among the children of men. For the law rules and governs mankind. Therefore the law judges mankind, and not mankind the law.

If Christ be not God, then neither the Father nor the Holy Spirit is God; for our article of faith speaks thus: "Christ is God, with the Father and the Holy Spirit." Many there are who talk much of the Godhead of Christ, but they speak as a blind man speaks of colors. Therefore, when I hear Christ speak, and say, "Come to me, all ye that are weary and heavy laden, and I will give you rest," then do I believe steadfastly that the whole Godhead speaks in an undivided and unseparated substance. He that preaches a God to me that died not for me the death on the cross, that God will I not receive.

He that has this article has the chief and principal article of faith, though to the world it seems unmeaning and ridiculous. Christ says, "The Comforter which I will send shall not depart from you, but will remain with you, and will make you able to endure all manner of tribulations and evil." When Christ says, "I will pray to the Father," then he speaks as a human creature, or as very man. But when he says he will do this or that, as before he said, "I will send the Comforter," then he speaks as very God. In this manner do I learn my article, "That Christ is both God and man."

I, out of my own experience, am able to witness that Jesus Christ is true God; I know full well and have found what the name of Jesus has done for me. I have often been so near death that I thought now must I die because I teach his Word to the wicked world and acknowledge him. But always he mercifully put life into me, refreshed and comforted me. Therefore, let us use diligence to only follow him, and then all is safe, although the devil were ever so wicked and crafty, and the world ever so evil and false. Whatever happens to me, I will surely cleave to my sweet Saviour Christ Jesus, for in him am I baptized. I cannot do or know anything but only what he has taught me.

The Holy Scriptures, especially those written by Paul, ascribe to Christ that which he gives to the Father, namely, the divine almighty power; so that he can give grace, peace of conscience, forgiveness of sins, life, and victory over sin, death, and the devil. Now, unless Paul would rob God of his honor and give it to another that is not God, he dared not ascribe such properties and attributes to Christ if he were not true God; and God himself says, "I will not give my glory to another." And, indeed, no man can give that to another which he has not himself. But seeing that Christ gives grace and peace, the Holy Spirit also, and redeems from the power of the devil, sin, and death, so is it most sure that he has an endless, immeasurable, almighty power, equal with the Father.

Christ brings peace, but not as the apostles brought it, through preaching; he gives it as a Creator to his creature. The Father creates and gives life, grace, and peace; and even so gives the Son the same gifts. Now, to give grace, peace, everlasting life, forgiveness of sins, and to justify, save, and deliver from death and hell, surely these are not the works of any creature but of the sole majesty of God, things which the angels themselves can neither create nor give. Therefore, such works pertain to the high majesty, honor, and glory of God, who is the only and true Creator of all things.

God who speaks not out of Christ's mouth is not God. God, in the Old Testament, bound himself to the throne of grace; there was the place where he would hear, so long as the policy and government of Moses stood and flourished. In like manner, he will still hear no man or human creature, except through Christ. As a number of the Jews ran to and fro, burning incense and offerings here and there, and seeking God in various places, not regarding the tabernacle, so it goes now: we seek God everywhere; but not seeking him in Christ, we find him nowhere.

—Of Jesus Christ

QUESTIONS TO CONSIDER
1. How can we see Jesus as both fully man and fully God?
2. Why is this important to understand?

A PRAYERFUL RESPONSE
Lord, thank you for becoming human to save us from sin. Amen.

The Holy Spirit in Us

THOUGHT FOR TODAY

The Holy Spirit assures us of our place in God's family.

WISDOM FROM SCRIPTURE

Then Peter, filled with the Holy Spirit, said to them: "Rulers and elders of the people!

"If we are being called to account today for an act of kindness shown to a cripple and are asked how he was healed, then know this, you and all the people of Israel: It is by the name of Jesus Christ of Nazareth, whom you crucified but whom God raised from the dead, that this man stands before you healed.

"He is 'the stone you builders rejected, which has become the capstone.'

"Salvation is found in no one else, for there is no other name under heaven given to men by which we must be saved."

When they saw the courage of Peter and John and realized that they were unschooled, ordinary men, they were astonished and they took note that these men had been with Jesus.

But since they could see the man who had been healed standing there with them, there was nothing they could say.

ACTS 4:8-14, NIV

INSIGHTS FROM MARTIN LUTHER

The Holy Spirit has two offices. First, he is a Spirit of grace that makes God gracious unto us and receives us as his acceptable children, for Christ's sake. Secondly, he is a Spirit of prayer that prays for us and for the whole world, to the end that all evil may be turned from us and that all good may happen to us. The Spirit of grace teaches people; the Spirit of prayer prays. It is a wonder how one thing is accomplished various ways. It is one thing to have the Holy Spirit as a spirit of prophecy, and another to have the revealing of the same; for many have had the Holy Spirit before the birth of Christ, and yet he was not revealed to them.

We do not separate the Holy Spirit from faith; neither do we teach that he is against faith; for he is the certainty itself in the world, that makes us sure and certain of the Word so that, without all wavering or doubting, we certainly believe that everything is as God's Word says and is delivered to us. But the Holy Spirit is given to none without the Word.

There are those who have no certainty at all; neither can they be sure of these things, for they depend not on God's Word but on their own righteousness. And when they have done many and great works, yet they always stand in doubt and say: Who knows whether this which we have done be pleasing to God or not; or whether we have done enough works or not? They must continually think within themselves, *We are still unworthy.*

But a true and godly Christian, between these two doubts, is sure and certain, and says: I do not regard these doubts; I neither look upon my holiness nor upon my unworthiness, but I believe in Jesus Christ, who is both holy and worthy. I am sure and certain that Christ gives himself, with all his holiness, worthiness, and what he is and has, to be mine own. For my part, I am a poor sinner, sure of God's Word. Therefore, the Holy Spirit only and alone is able to say: Jesus Christ is the

Lord; the Holy Spirit teaches, preaches, and declares Christ.

The Holy Spirit goes first and before in what pertains to teaching; but in what concerns hearing, the Word goes first and before, and then the Holy Spirit follows after. For we must first hear the Word, and then afterwards the Holy Spirit works in our hearts. He works in the hearts of whom he will, and how he will, but never without the Word.

The Holy Spirit began his office and his work openly on Whitsunday [Pentecost]; for he gave to the apostles and disciples of Christ a true and certain comfort in their hearts, and a secure and joyful courage in such a measure that they regarded not whether the world and the devil were merry or sad, friends or enemies, angry or pleased. They went in all security up and down the streets of the city, and doubtless they had these or like thoughts: We regard neither Annas or Caiaphas, Pilate nor Herod; they have nothing over us; they are our subjects and servants, we their lords and rulers. So went the loving apostles on, in all courage, without seeking leave or license.

They asked not whether they should preach, or whether the priests and people would allow it. O, no! They went on boldly; they opened their mouths freely and reproved all the people, rulers and subjects, as murderers, wicked wretches, and traitors, who had slain the Prince of Life.

Therefore the Whitsuntide sermons of the Holy Spirit [the week following Whitsunday] are very needful for us, that thereby we may be comforted and with boldness condemn and slight such blaspheming, and that the Holy Spirit may put boldness and courage into our hearts that we may stoutly thrust ourselves forward. Let who will be offended, and let who will reproach us. Although sects and heresies arise, we may not regard them. Such a courage there must be that cares for nothing, but boldly and freely acknowledges and preaches Christ, who of wicked hands was crucified and slain.

The preached gospel is offensive in all places of the world, rejected and condemned. If the gospel did not offend and anger citizen or countryman, prince or bishop, then it would be a fine and acceptable preaching, and might well be tolerated, and people would willingly hear and receive it. But seeing it is a kind of preaching which makes people angry, especially the great and powerful, and deep-learned ones of the world, great courage is necessary, and the Holy Spirit, to those that intend to preach it. Thus it is with the church of Christ: It goes on in apparent weakness; and yet in its weakness there is such mighty strength and power that all the worldly-wise and powerful must stand amazed and afraid.

It is testified by Holy Scripture—and the Nicene creed out of Holy Scripture teaches—that the Holy Spirit is he who makes alive and, together with the Father and the Son, is worshiped and glorified.

Therefore, the Holy Spirit, of necessity, must be true and everlasting God with the Father and the Son—one essence. For if he were not true and everlasting God, then could not be attributed and given unto him the divine power and honor that he makes alive. Together with the Father and the Son he is worshiped and glorified.

The Holy Spirit is not such a comforter as the world is, where neither truth nor constancy is, but he is a true, everlasting, and constant comforter, without deceit and lies. He is one whom no man can deceive. He is called a witness because he bears witness only of Christ and of none other. Without his testimony concerning Christ, there is no true or firm comfort. Therefore, all rests on this, that we take sure hold of the text and say: I believe in Jesus Christ, who died for me; and I know that the Holy Spirit, who is called, and is a witness and a comforter, preaches and witnesses in Christendom of none but Christ, therewith to strengthen and comfort all sad and sorrowful hearts. There will I also remain, depending upon none other for comfort.

Our blessed Saviour, Christ himself, preaches that the Holy Spirit is everlasting and Almighty God. Otherwise he would not have directed his commission thus: "Go, and teach all nations, and baptize them in the name of the Father, of the Son, and of the Holy Spirit, and teach them to keep and observe all things whatsoever I have commanded of you." It must needs follow that the Holy Spirit is true eternal God, equal in power and might with the Father, and the Son, without end.

Likewise, Christ says: "And I will pray the Father, and he shall give you another comforter, that he may abide with you forever; even the Spirit of Truth, whom the world cannot receive, because it sees him not, neither knows him." Mark well this sentence, for herein we find the difference of the three persons distinctly held out unto us: "I will pray the Father, and he shall give you another comforter." Here we have two persons—Christ the Son that prays, and the Father that is prayed to.

Now, if the Father shall give such a comforter, then the Father himself cannot be that comforter; neither can Christ, who prays, be the same. The three persons are here plainly pictured and portrayed unto us. For even as the Father and the Son are two distinct persons, so the third person of the Holy Spirit is another distinct person, and yet notwithstanding there is but one only everlasting God.

—Of the Holy Ghost

QUESTIONS TO CONSIDER
1. What is the role of the Holy Spirit in your life?
2. How do you need the Holy Spirit to empower you?

A PRAYERFUL RESPONSE
Lord, show me the strength and comfort of your Holy Spirit. Amen.

What Is Faith?

THOUGHT FOR TODAY

Faith is a living trust in God's grace.

WISDOM FROM SCRIPTURE

As for you, you were dead in your transgressions and sins, in which you used to live when you followed the ways of this world and of the ruler of the kingdom of the air, the spirit who is now at work in those who are disobedient.

All of us also lived among them at one time, gratifying the cravings of our sinful nature and following its desires and thoughts. Like the rest, we were by nature objects of wrath.

But because of his great love for us, God, who is rich in mercy, made us alive with Christ even when we were dead in transgressions—it is by grace you have been saved.

And God raised us up with Christ and seated us with him in the heavenly realms in Christ Jesus, in order that in the coming ages he might show the incomparable riches of his grace, expressed in his kindness to us in Christ Jesus.

For it is by grace you have been saved, through faith—and this not from yourselves, it is the gift of God—not by works, so that no one can boast.

For we are God's workmanship, created in Christ Jesus to do good works, which God prepared in advance for us to do.

Therefore, remember that formerly you who are Gentiles by birth and called "uncircumcised" by those who call themselves "the circumcision" (that done in the body by the hands of men)—remember that at that time you were separate from Christ, excluded from citizenship in Israel and foreigners to the covenants of the promise, without hope and without God in the world.

But now in Christ Jesus you who once were far away have been brought near through the blood of Christ.

EPHESIANS 2:1-13, NIV

INSIGHTS FROM MARTIN LUTHER

Faith is not what some people think it is. Their human dream is a delusion. Because they observe that faith is not followed by good works or a better life, they fall into error, even though they speak and hear much about faith.

"Faith is not enough," they say, "You must do good works, you must be pious to be saved."

They think that when you hear the gospel, you start working, creating by your own strength a thankful heart which says, "I believe."

That is what they think true faith is. But because this is a human idea, a dream, the heart never learns anything from it, so it does nothing and reform doesn't come from this "faith," either.

Instead, faith is God's work in us, that changes us and gives new birth from God (see John 1:13). It kills the Old Adam and makes us completely different people. It changes our hearts, our spirits, our thoughts, and all our powers. It brings the Holy Spirit with it.

Yes, it is a living, creative, active, and powerful thing, this faith. Faith cannot help doing good works constantly. It doesn't stop to ask if good works ought to be done, but before anyone asks, it already has done them and continues to do them without ceasing. Anyone who does not do good works in this manner is an unbeliever. He stumbles around and looks for faith and good works, even though he does not know what faith or good works are. Yet he gossips and chatters about faith and good works with many words.

Faith is a living, bold trust in God's grace, so certain of God's favor that it would risk death a thousand times trusting in it. Such confidence and knowledge of God's grace makes you happy, joyful, and bold in your relationship to God and all creatures. The Spirit makes this happen through faith. Because of it, you freely, willingly, and joyfully do good to everyone, serve everyone, suffer all kinds of things, and love and praise the God who has shown you such grace. Thus, it is just as impossible to separate faith and works as it is to separate heat and light from fire!

Therefore, watch out for your own false ideas and guard against good-for-nothing gossips, who think they're smart enough to define faith and works, but really are the greatest of fools.

Ask God to work faith in you, or you will remain forever without faith, no matter what you wish, say, or can do.

—An Introduction to St. Paul's Letter to the Romans

QUESTIONS TO CONSIDER

1. Have you received salvation by faith? How do you know?
2. How could your faith be demonstrated through action?

A PRAYERFUL RESPONSE

Lord, work faith into my heart and life today. Amen.

DAY 6

Faith Versus the Law

It requires faith to fulfill the law.

WISDOM FROM SCRIPTURE

Now you, if you call yourself a Jew; if you rely on the law and brag about your relationship to God; if you know his will and approve of what is superior because you are instructed by the law; if you are convinced that you are a guide for the blind, a light for those who are in the dark, an instructor of the foolish, a teacher of infants, because you have in the law the embodiment of knowledge and truth—you, then, who teach others, do you not teach yourself? You who preach against stealing, do you steal?

You who say that people should not commit adultery, do you commit adultery? You who abhor idols, do you rob temples?

You who brag about the law, do you dishonor God by breaking the law?

A man is not a Jew if he is only one outwardly, nor is circumcision merely outward and physical.

No, a man is a Jew if he is one inwardly; and circumcision is circumcision of the heart, by the Spirit, not by the written code. Such a man's praise is not from men, but from God.

ROMANS 2:17-23; 28-29, NIV

God judges what is in the depths of the heart. Therefore, his law also makes demands on the depths of the heart and doesn't let the heart rest content in works; rather it punishes as hypocrisy and lies all works done apart from the depths of the heart. All human beings are liars, since none of them keep or can keep God's law from the depths of the heart. Everyone finds inside himself an aversion to good and a craving for evil. Where there is no free desire for good, there the heart has not set itself on God's law. There also sin is surely to be found and the deserved wrath of God, whether a lot of good works and an honorable life appear outwardly or not.

Outwardly you keep the law with works out of fear of punishment or love of gain. Likewise, you do everything without free desire and love of the law; you act out of aversion and force. You'd rather act otherwise if the law didn't exist. It follows, then, that you, in the depths of your heart, are an enemy of the law. What do you mean, therefore, by teaching another not to steal, when you, in the depths of your heart, are a thief and would be one outwardly too, if you dared? So then, you teach others but not yourself; you don't even know what you are teaching. You've never understood the law rightly. Furthermore, the law increases sin, as Paul says. That is because a person becomes more and more an enemy of the law the more it demands of him what he can't possibly do.

Paul also says the law is spiritual. What does that mean? If the law were physical, then it could be satisfied by works, but since it is spiritual, no one can satisfy it unless everything he does springs from the depths of the heart. But no one can give such a heart except the Spirit of God, who makes the person be like the law, so that he actually conceives a heartfelt longing for the law and henceforward does everything, not through fear or coercion, but from a free heart. Such a law is spiritual since it can only be loved and fulfilled by such a heart and such a spirit. If the Spirit is not in the heart, then there remains sin, aversion, and enmity against the law, which in itself is good, just, and holy.

You must get used to the idea that it is one thing to do the works of the law and quite another to fulfill it. The works of the law are everything that a person does or can do of his own free will and by his own powers to obey the law. But because in doing such works the heart abhors the law and yet is forced to obey it, the works are a total loss and are completely useless.

But to fulfill the law means to do its work eagerly, lovingly, and freely, without the constraint of the law; it means to live well and in a manner pleasing to God, as though there were no law or punishment. It is the Holy Spirit, however, who puts such eagerness of unconstrained love into the heart. But the Spirit is given only in, with, and through faith in Jesus Christ. So, too, faith comes only through the Word of God, the gospel, that preaches Christ: how he is both Son of God and man, how he died and rose for our sake.

That is why faith alone makes someone just and fulfills the law; faith brings the Holy Spirit through the merits of Christ. The Spirit, in turn, renders the heart glad and free, as the law demands. Then good works proceed from faith itself. That is what Paul means when, after he has thrown out the works of the law, he sounds as though he wants to abolish the law by faith. No, he says, we uphold the law through faith; we fulfill it through faith.

This is what the Holy Spirit does by faith. Through faith, a person will do good to everyone without coercion—willingly and happily; he will serve everyone, suffer everything for the love and praise of God, who has shown him such grace. It is as impossible to separate works from faith as to separate burning and shining from fire. Therefore, be on guard against your own false ideas and against the chatterers who think they are clever enough to make judgments about faith and good works but who are in reality the biggest fools. Ask God to work faith in you; otherwise you will remain eternally without faith, no matter what you try to do or fabricate.

—Preface to the Letter of St. Paul to the Romans

QUESTIONS TO CONSIDER

1. What is the difference between obeying the law and fulfilling it?
2. How can you fulfill the law through faith?

A PRAYERFUL RESPONSE

Lord, please give me a desire to fulfill your law through faith. Amen.

DAY 7

Faith Versus Works

Even our best works originate through God's grace.

WISDOM FROM SCRIPTURE

If, in fact, Abraham was justified by works, he had something to boast about—but not before God.

What does the Scripture say? "Abraham believed God, and it was credited to him as righteousness."

Now when a man works, his wages are not credited to him as a gift, but as an obligation.

However, to the man who does not work but trusts God who justifies the wicked, his faith is credited as righteousness.

David says the same thing when he speaks of the blessedness of the man to whom God credits righteousness apart from works: "Blessed are they whose transgressions are forgiven, whose sins are covered.

"Blessed is the man whose sin the Lord will never count against him."

ROMANS 4:2-8, NIV

INSIGHTS FROM MARTIN LUTHER

We ought first to know that there are no good works except those which God has commanded, even as there is no sin except that which God has forbidden. Therefore, whoever wishes to know and to do good works needs nothing else than to know God's commandments. Thus Christ says, "If thou wilt enter into life, keep the commandments." And when the young man asks him what he shall do that he may inherit eternal life, Christ sets before him naught else but the Ten Commandments. Accordingly, we must learn how to distinguish among good works from the Commandments of God, and not from the appearance, the magnitude, the number of the works themselves, or from the judgment of men or of human law or custom, as we see has been done and still is done because we are blind and despise the divine Commandments.

The first and highest, the most precious of all good works is faith in Christ, as he says when the Jews asked him: "What shall we do that we may work the works of God?" He answered: "This is the work of God, that ye believe on him whom he hath sent." When we hear or preach this word, we hasten over it and deem it a very little thing and easy to do, whereas we ought to pause a long time and to ponder it well. For in this work all good works must be done and receive from it the inflow of their goodness, like a loan. This we must say bluntly, that men may understand it.

Now everyone can note and tell for himself when he does what is good or what is not good; for if he finds his heart confident that it pleases God, the work is good, even if it were so small a thing as picking up a straw. If confidence is absent, or if he doubts, the work is not good, although it should raise all the dead and the man should give himself to be burned. This is the teaching of Paul: "Whatsoever is not done of or in faith is sin." Faith, as the chief work, and no other work, has given us the name of "believers on Christ." For all other works a heathen, a Jew, a sinner, may also do; but to trust firmly that he pleases God is possible only for a Christian who is enlightened and strengthened by grace.

—*A Treatise on Good Works*

QUESTIONS TO CONSIDER
1. Why do we try to work our way into God's grace?
2. How do faith and works complement each other?

A PRAYERFUL RESPONSE
Lord, teach me how to live by faith and not works. Amen.

The Nature of Sin

THOUGHT FOR TODAY

We are all sinners, saved only by the grace of God.

WISDOM FROM SCRIPTURE

As it is written: "There is no one righteous, not even one; there is no one who understands, no one who seeks God.

"All have turned away, they have together become worthless; there is no one who does good, not even one."

"Their throats are open graves; their tongues practice deceit."

"The poison of vipers is on their lips."

"Their mouths are full of cursing and bitterness."

"Their feet are swift to shed blood; ruin and misery mark their ways, and the way of peace they do not know."

"There is no fear of God before their eyes."

Now we know that whatever the law says, it says to those who are under the law, so that every mouth may be silenced and the whole world held accountable to God.

Therefore no one will be declared righteous in his sight by observing the law; rather, through the law we become conscious of sin.

But now a righteousness from God, apart from law, has been made known, to which the Law and the Prophets testify.

This righteousness from God comes through faith in Jesus Christ to all who believe. There is no difference, for all have sinned and fall short of the glory of God, and are justified freely by his grace through the redemption that came by Christ Jesus.

ROMANS 3:10-24, NIV

INSIGHTS FROM MARTIN LUTHER

We are all sinners by nature—conceived and born in sin; sin has poisoned us through and through. We have from Adam a will that continually sets itself against God, unless by the Holy Spirit it be renewed and changed.

No man understands or feels these sins, but he that has the Holy Spirit and the grace of God. Therefore, people feel secure, though they draw God's wrath upon them, yet flatter themselves they still remain in God's favor. They corrupt the Word of God and condemn it; yet think they do that which is pleasing and a special service to God.

For example, Paul held the law of God to be the highest and most precious treasure on earth, as we do the gospel. He would venture life and blood to maintain it; and he thought he lacked neither understanding, wisdom, nor power. But before he could rightly look about him, and while he thought his cause most sure, then he heard another lesson, he got another manner of commission, and it was told him plainly that all his works, actions, diligence, and zeal were quite against God. Yet his doings carried a fair favor with the learned and seemingly holy people who said, "Paul dealt herein uprightly and performed divine and holy works in showing such zeal for God's honor and for the law." But God struck him and he fell to the ground and heard, 'Saul, Saul, why persecutest thou me?' As if Christ should say, "Saul, even with that wherein you think to do me service, you do nothing but persecute me, as my greatest enemy."

Christ well knew how to discriminate sins; we see in the gospel how harsh he was toward the Pharisees, by reason of their great hatred and envy against him and his Word, while, on the contrary, how mild and friendly he was toward the woman who was a sinner. That same envy will rob Christ of his Word, for he is a bitter enemy unto it, and in the end will crucify it. But the woman, as the greatest sinner, takes hold on the Word, hears Christ, and believes that he is the only Saviour of the world; she washes his feet and anoints him with costly perfume.

Let us not think ourselves more just than was the poor sinner and murderer on the cross. I believe if the apostles had not fallen, they would not have believed in the remission of sins. Therefore, when the devil upbraids me, touching my sins, then I say: *Although I am a great sinner, yet I have not denied Christ my Saviour, as you did.* In such instances the forgiveness of sins remains confirmed. And although the apostles were sinners, yet our Saviour Christ always excused them, as when they plucked the ears of corn. But he jeered the Pharisees touching the paying of tribute and frequently showed his disapprobation of them. The disciples he always comforted, as Peter, where he says: "Fear not, thou shalt henceforth catch men."

No sinner can escape his punishment unless he be sorry for his sins. For though one go scot-free for awhile, yet at last he will be snapped, as the Psalm says: "God indeed is still judge on earth."

God forgives sins merely out of grace for Christ's sake; but we must not abuse the grace of God. God has given signs and tokens enough that our sins shall be forgiven; namely, the preaching of the gospel, baptism, the Lord's Supper, and the Holy Spirit in our hearts.

Now it is also needful that we testify in our works that we have received the forgiveness of sins by each forgiving the faults of his brother. There is no comparison between God's remitting of sins and ours. For what are one hundred pence in comparison with ten thousand pounds? As Christ says, nothing. And although we deserve nothing by our forgiving, yet we must forgive, that in doing so we may prove and give testimony that we from God have received forgiveness of our sins.

The forgiveness of sins is declared only in God's Word, and there we must seek it; for it is grounded on God's promises. God forgives your sins not because you feel them and are sorry, for this, sin itself produces, without deserving. He forgives your sins because he is merciful and has promised to forgive for Christ's sake.

It can be hurtful to none to acknowledge and confess his sins. Have you done this or that sin?—what then? We freely, in God's name, acknowledge the same and deny it not, but from our hearts say: O Lord God! I have done this sin.

Original sin, after regeneration, is like a wound that begins to heal; though it be a wound, yet it is in the process of healing, though it still runs and is sore. So original sin remains in Christians until they die, yet itself is mortified and continually dying. Its head is crushed in pieces so that it cannot condemn us.

—Of Sins

QUESTIONS TO CONSIDER

1. How can you develop a habit of confessing your sins?
2. How does sin make us all equal in the sight of God?

A PRAYERFUL RESPONSE

Lord, thank you for forgiving my sins as I confess them to you.
Amen.

DAY 9

Our Free Will

There is nothing good in us apart from Christ.

WISDOM FROM SCRIPTURE

For it is written: "I will destroy the wisdom of the wise; the intelligence of the intelligent I will frustrate."

Where is the wise man? Where is the scholar? Where is the philosopher of this age? Has not God made foolish the wisdom of the world?

For since in the wisdom of God the world through its wisdom did not know him, God was pleased through the foolishness of what was preached to save those who believe.

Jews demand miraculous signs and Greeks look for wisdom, but we preach Christ crucified: a stumbling block to Jews and foolishness to Gentiles, but to those whom God has called, both Jews and Greeks, Christ the power of God and the wisdom of God.

For the foolishness of God is wiser than man's wisdom, and the weakness of God is stronger than man's strength.

Brothers, think of what you were when you were called. Not many of you were wise by human standards; not many were influential; not many were of noble birth.

But God chose the foolish things of the world to shame the wise; God chose the weak things of the world to shame the strong.

He chose the lowly things of this world and the despised

things—and the things that are not—to nullify the things that are, so that no one may boast before him.

It is because of him that you are in Christ Jesus, who has become for us wisdom from God—that is, our righteousness, holiness and redemption.

Therefore, as it is written: "Let him who boasts boast in the Lord."

1 CORINTHIANS 1:19-31, NIV

INSIGHTS FROM MARTIN LUTHER

I, for my part, admit that God gave to mankind a free will, but the question is whether this same freedom produces our power and strength, or not? We may very fitly call it a subverted, perverse, fickle, and wavering will, for it is only God that works in us, and we must suffer and be subject to his pleasure. Even as a potter makes a pot or vessel as he wills, so it is for our free will to suffer and not to work. It stands not in our strength; for we are not able to do anything that is good in divine matters.

I have often resolved to live uprightly and to lead a godly life, and to set everything aside that would hinder this. But it was far from being put in execution, even as it was with Peter, when he swore he would lay down his life for Christ. I will not lie before my God but will freely confess that I am not able to effect that good which I intend. I await the happy hour when God shall be pleased to meet me with his grace.

The will of mankind is either presumptuous or despairing. No human creature can satisfy the law. For the law of God discourses with me, as it were, after this manner: Here is a high, steep mountain, and you must go over it; when I hear this my flesh and free will say, "I will go over it"; but my conscience says, "You cannot go over it." Then comes despair, and says, "If I cannot, then I must forbear." In this sort does the law work in mankind either presumption or despair; yet the law must be preached and taught, for if we preach not the law, then people grow rude and confident. But if we preach it, we make them afraid.

Man, without the Holy Spirit and God's grace, can do nothing but sin; he proceeds therein without intermission, and from one sin falls into another. Now, if man will not suffer wholesome doctrine, but condemns the all-saving Word and resists the Holy Spirit, then through the effects and strength of his free will he becomes God's enemy. He blasphemes the Holy Spirit and follows the lusts and desires of his own heart, as examples throughout history clearly show.

But we must diligently weigh the words the Holy Spirit speaks through Moses: "Every imagination of the thoughts of his heart is evil continually," so that everything a man is able to conceive with his thoughts, with his understanding and free will, by highest diligence, is evil, and not once or twice, but evil continually. Without the Holy Spirit, man's reason, will, and understanding are without the knowledge of God; and to be without the knowledge of God is nothing else than to be ungodly, to walk in darkness, and to hold those things as best that are in direct opposition to the best.

I speak only of that which is good in divine things and according to the Holy Scripture. We must make a difference between that which is temporal and that which is spiritual, between politics and divinity; for God also allows good of the government of the ungodly and rewards their virtues, yet only so far as belongs to this temporal life. Man's will and understanding conceive that to be good which is external and temporal—nay, take it to be, not only good but the chief good.

When we speak of free will, we ask what man's free will is able to accomplish in divine and spiritual matters. We conclude that man, without the Holy Spirit, is altogether wicked before God, although he were decked up and trimmed with all the virtues of the heathen and had all their works. For, indeed, there are fair and glorious examples in heathendom of many virtues, where men were temperate, chaste, bountiful; loved their country, parents, wives, and children; were men of courage and behaved themselves magnanimously and generously.

Ah, Lord God! Why should we boast of our free will as if it were able to do anything ever so small in divine and spiritual matters? When we consider what horrible miseries the devil has brought upon us through sin, we might shame ourselves to death.

O! How excellent and comfortable a gospel is that in which our Saviour Christ shows what a loving heart he bears toward us poor sinners who are able to do nothing at all for ourselves for our salvation.

—Of Free Will

QUESTIONS TO CONSIDER

1. Why is it difficult to admit that we're not capable of good on our own?
2. How can you rely on the Holy Spirit to lead a godly life?

A PRAYERFUL RESPONSE

Lord, I want to be acceptable in your sight. Amen.

DAY 10

The True Gospel

THOUGHT FOR TODAY
God's true gospel is based on his salvation through faith alone.

WISDOM FROM SCRIPTURE
Some false brothers had infiltrated our ranks to spy on the freedom we have in Christ Jesus and to make us slaves.

We did not give in to them for a moment, so that the truth of the gospel might remain with you.

As for those who seemed to be important—whatever they were makes no difference to me; God does not judge by external appearance—those men added nothing to my message.

On the contrary, they saw that I had been entrusted with the task of preaching the gospel to the Gentiles, just as Peter had been to the Jews.

For God, who was at work in the ministry of Peter as an apostle to the Jews, was also at work in my ministry as an apostle to the Gentiles.

James, Peter, and John, those reputed to be pillars, gave me and Barnabas the right hand of fellowship when they recognized the grace given to me. They agreed that we should go to the Gentiles, and they to the Jews.

All they asked was that we should continue to remember the poor, the very thing I was eager to do.

When Peter came to Antioch, I opposed him to his face, because he was clearly in the wrong.

Before certain men came from James, he used to eat with

the Gentiles. But when they arrived, he began to draw back and separate himself from the Gentiles because he was afraid of those who belonged to the circumcision group.

The other Jews joined him in his hypocrisy, so that by their hypocrisy even Barnabas was led astray.

GALATIANS 2:4-13, NIV

INSIGHTS FROM MARTIN LUTHER

Paul explains his motive for going up to Jerusalem. He did not go to Jerusalem to be instructed or confirmed in his gospel by the other apostles. He went to Jerusalem in order to preserve the true gospel for the Galatian churches and for all the churches of the Gentiles.

When Paul speaks of the truth of the gospel he implies by contrast a false gospel. The false apostles also had a gospel, but it was an untrue gospel. "In holding out against them," says Paul, "I conserved the truth of the pure gospel."

Now the true gospel has it that we are justified by faith alone, without the deeds of the law. The false gospel has it that we are justified by faith, but not without the deeds of the law. The false apostles preached a conditional gospel. They admitted that faith is the foundation of salvation. But they added the conditional clause that faith can save only when it is furnished with good works. This is wrong. The true gospel declares that good works are the embellishment of faith, but that faith itself is the gift and work of God in our hearts. Faith is able to justify because it apprehends Christ, the Redeemer.

Human reason can think only in terms of the law. It mumbles: "This I have done, this I have not done." But faith looks to Jesus Christ, the Son of God, given unto death for the sins of the whole world. To turn one's eyes away from Jesus means to turn them to the law.

True faith lays hold of Christ and leans on him alone. Our opponents cannot understand this. In their blindness they cast away the precious pearl, Christ, and hang on to their stubborn works. They have no idea what faith is. How can they teach faith to others?

Not satisfied with teaching an untrue gospel, the false apostles tried to entangle Paul. "They went about," says Paul, "to spy out our liberty which we have in Christ Jesus, that they might bring us into bondage."

When Paul saw through their scheme, he attacked the false apostles. He says, "We did not let go of the liberty which we have in Christ Jesus. We routed them by the judgment of the apostles, and we would not give in to them, no, not an inch."

Likewise, we will not give up the liberty of conscience we have in Christ Jesus. We refuse to have our conscience bound by any work or law, so that by doing this or that we should be righteous, or leaving this or that undone we should be damned.

Since our opponents will not let it stand that only faith in Christ justifies, we will not yield to them. On the question of justification we must remain adamant or else we shall lose the truth of the gospel. It is a matter of life and death. It involves the death of the Son of God, who died for the sins of the world. If we surrender faith in Christ as the only thing that can justify us, the death and resurrection of Jesus are without meaning; Christ as the Saviour of the world would be a myth. God would be a liar because he would not have fulfilled his promises.

Our stubbornness is right because we want to preserve the liberty we have in Christ. Only by preserving our liberty shall we be able to retain the truth of the gospel.

When the conscience is disturbed, do not seek advice from reason or from the law, but rest your conscience in the grace of God and in his Word, and proceed as if you had never heard of the law. The law has its place and its own good time. While Moses was on the mountain where he talked with God face to face, he had no law, he made no law, he administered no law. But when he came down from the mountain, he was a law-giver. The conscience must be kept above the law, the body under the law.

Paul reproved Peter for no trifle but for the chief article of Christian doctrine, which Peter's hypocrisy had endangered. For Barnabas and other Jews followed Peter's example. It is surprising that such good men as Peter, Barnabas, and others should fall into unexpected error, especially in a matter which they knew so well. To trust in our own strength, our own goodness, our own wisdom, is a perilous thing. Let us search the Scriptures with humility, praying that we may never lose the light of the gospel. "Lord, increase our faith."

—Commentary on the Epistle to the Galatians

QUESTIONS TO CONSIDER

1. How can you discern when a "false gospel" is being taught?
2. Why do you think Martin Luther was so emphatic that the true gospel is "justification by faith alone"?

A PRAYERFUL RESPONSE

Lord, I need discernment to know your true gospel. Amen.

PART TWO

Living in Righteousness

Lord, keep us steadfast in thy Word;
Curb those who fain by craft and sword
Would wrest the Kingdom from thy Son
And set at naught all he hath done.

Lord Jesus Christ, thy power make known,
For thou art Lord of lords alone;
Defend thy Christendom that we
May evermore sing praise to thee.

O Comforter of priceless worth,
Send peace and unity on earth.
Support us in our final strife
And lead us out of death to life.

From "Lord, Keep Us Steadfast in Thy Word"
by Martin Luther

MARTIN LUTHER'S INSIGHT
Living by faith requires walking in righteousness.

The Justice of God

THOUGHT FOR TODAY

A just person lives by faith.

WISDOM FROM SCRIPTURE

Therefore, since we are justified by faith, we have peace with God through our Lord Jesus Christ, through whom we have obtained access to this grace in which we stand; and we boast in our hope of sharing the glory of God.

And not only that, but we also boast in our sufferings, knowing that suffering produces endurance, and endurance produces character, and character produces hope, and hope does not disappoint us, because God's love has been poured into our hearts through the Holy Spirit that has been given to us.

For while we were still weak, at the right time Christ died for the ungodly.

Indeed, rarely will anyone die for a righteous person— though perhaps for a good person someone might actually dare to die.

But God proves his love for us in that while we still were sinners Christ died for us.

Much more surely then, now that we have been justified by his blood, will we be saved through him from the wrath of God.

For if while we were enemies, we were reconciled to God through the death of his Son, much more surely, having been reconciled, will we be saved by his life.

But more than that, we even boast in God through our Lord Jesus Christ, through whom we have now received reconciliation.

INSIGHTS FROM MARTIN LUTHER

In 1519, I had begun interpreting the Psalms once again. I felt confident that I was now more experienced, since I had dealt in university courses with Paul's Letters to the Romans, to the Galatians, and the Letter to the Hebrews. I had a burning desire to understand what Paul meant in his Letter to the Romans, but thus far there had stood in my way not the cold blood around my heart but the words in chapter one: "The justice of God is revealed in it." I hated those words, "justice of God," which, by the use and custom of all my teachers, I had been taught to understand philosophically as referring to formal or active justice, as they call it—that justice by which God is just and by which he punishes sinners and the unjust.

But I, blameless monk that I was, felt that before God I was a sinner with an extremely troubled conscience. I couldn't be sure that God was appeased by my satisfaction. I hated the just God who punishes sinners. In silence, if I did not blaspheme, then certainly I grumbled vehemently and got angry at God. I said, "Isn't it enough that we miserable sinners, lost for all eternity because of original sin, are oppressed by every kind of calamity through the Ten Commandments? Why does God heap sorrow upon sorrow through the gospel, and through the gospel threaten us with his justice and his wrath?" This was how I was raging with wild and disturbed conscience. I constantly badgered Paul about that spot in Romans 1 and anxiously wanted to know what he meant.

I meditated night and day on those words until at last, by the mercy of God, I paid attention to their context: "The justice of God is revealed in it, as it is written: 'The just person lives by faith.'" I began to understand that in this verse the justice of God is that by which the just person lives by a gift of God, that is by faith. I began to understand that this verse means that the justice of God is revealed through the gospel, but it is a passive justice—that by which the merciful God justifies us by faith, as it is written: "The just person lives by faith."

All at once I felt that I had been born again and entered into paradise itself through open gates. Immediately I saw the whole of Scripture in a different light. I ran through the Scriptures from memory and found that other terms had analogous meanings: the work of God, that is, what God works in us; the power of God, by which he makes us powerful; the wisdom of God, by which he makes us wise; the strength of God, the salvation of God, the glory of God.

I exalted these sweet words of mine, "the justice of God," with as much love as before I had hated it. This phrase of Paul's was for me the very gate of paradise. Afterward I read Augustine's "On the Spirit and the Letter," in which I found what I had not dared hope for. I discovered that he too interpreted "the justice of God" in a similar way, namely, as that with which God clothes us when he justifies us. Although Augustine had said it imperfectly and did not explain in detail how God imputes justice to us, still it pleased me that he taught the justice of God by which we are justified.

—*Preface to the Complete Edition of Luther's Latin Works*

QUESTIONS TO CONSIDER

1. How has God's merciful justice been revealed to you?
2. How does God's justice impact your life now?

A PRAYERFUL RESPONSE

Lord, thank you for the gift of merciful justice. Amen.

DAY 12

He Gave Himself

THOUGHT FOR TODAY
Christ's life and death were the payment for our sin.

WISDOM FROM SCRIPTURE
Grace to you and peace from God our Father and the Lord Jesus Christ, who gave himself for our sins to set us free from the present evil age, according to the will of our God and Father, to whom be the glory forever and ever. Amen.

I am astonished that you are so quickly deserting the one who called you in the grace of Christ and are turning to a different gospel—not that there is another gospel, but there are some who are confusing you and want to pervert the gospel of Christ.

But even if we or an angel from heaven should proclaim to you a gospel contrary to what we proclaimed to you, let that one be accursed!

As we have said before, so now I repeat, if anyone proclaims to you a gospel contrary to what you received, let that one be accursed!

Am I now seeking human approval, or God's approval? Or am I trying to please people? If I were still pleasing people I would not be a servant of Christ.

GALATIANS 1:3-10, NRSV

Paul sticks to his theme. He never loses sight of the purpose of his epistle. He does not say, "Who received our works," but, "Who gave." Gave what? Not gold or silver or paschal lambs or an angel, but himself. What for? Not for a crown or a kingdom or our goodness, but for our sins. These words are like so many thunderclaps of protest from heaven against every kind and type of self-merit. Underscore these words, for they are full of comfort for sore consciences.

How may we obtain remission of our sins? Paul answers: "The man who is named Jesus Christ and the Son of God gave himself for our sins." The heavy artillery of these words explodes works, merits, superstitions. For if our sins could be removed by our own efforts, what need was there for the Son of God to be given for them? Since Christ was given for our sins, it stands to reason that they cannot be put away by our own efforts.

This sentence also defines our sins as great. So great, in fact, that the whole world could not make amends for a single sin. The greatness of the ransom—Christ, the Son of God—indicates this. The vicious character of sin is brought out by the words "who gave himself for our sins." So vicious is sin that only the sacrifice of Christ could atone for sin. When we reflect that the one little word "sin" embraces the whole kingdom of Satan, and that it includes everything that is horrible, we have reason to tremble. But we are careless. We make light of sin. We think that by some little work or merit we can dismiss sin.

Note especially the pronoun "our" and its significance. We will readily agree that Christ gave himself for the sins of Peter, Paul, and others who were worthy of such grace. But feeling low, we find it hard to believe that Christ gave himself for our sins. We shy away from a personal application of the pronoun "our," and we refuse to have anything to do with God until we have made ourselves worthy by good deeds.

This attitude springs from a false concept of sin, the concept that sin is a small matter, easily taken care of by good works; that we must present ourselves unto God with a good conscience; that we must feel no sin before we may feel that Christ was given for our sins.

This attitude is universal and particularly developed in those who consider themselves better than others. Such people readily confess they are frequent sinners, but they regard their sins as of no such importance that they cannot easily be dissolved by some good action or would prevent them from appearing before the tribunal of Christ and demanding the reward of eternal life for their righteousness. Meantime they pretend great humility and acknowledge a certain degree of sinfulness for which they soulfully join in the publican's prayer, "God, be merciful to me, a sinner." But the real significance and comfort of the words "for our sins" is lost upon them.

The genius of Christianity takes the words of Paul, "who gave himself for our sins," as true and efficacious. We are not to look upon our sins as insignificant trifles. On the other hand, we are not to regard them as so terrible that we must despair. Learn to believe that Christ was given, not for small or imaginary transgressions, but for mountainous sins. Not for one or two, but for all. Not for sins that can be discarded, but for sins that are stubbornly ingrained.

Practice this knowledge and fortify yourself against despair, particularly in the last hour, when the memory of past sins assails the conscience. Say with confidence: "Christ, the Son of God, was given not for the righteous, but for sinners. If I had no sin I should not need Christ. No, Satan, you cannot delude me into thinking I am holy. The truth is, I am all sin. My sins are not imaginary transgressions, but sins of unbelief, doubt, despair, contempt, hatred, ignorance of God, ingratitude towards him, misuse of his name, neglect of his Word. My sins include dishonor of parents, disobedience of government, and coveting of another's possessions. Granted that I have not committed murder, adultery, theft, and similar sins in deed, nevertheless, I have committed them in the heart, and therefore I am a transgressor of all the commandments of God. Because my transgressions are multiplied and my own efforts at self-justification are a hindrance, Christ the Son of God gave himself into death for my sins."

To believe this is to have eternal life.

—*Commentary on the Epistle to the Galatians*

QUESTIONS TO CONSIDER

1. Have you received Christ's death as payment for your debt of sin?
2. Do you ever view your sin as an "imaginary transgression"?

A PRAYERFUL RESPONSE

Lord, show me the magnitude of the sin in my life. Amen.

Justified by Christ

THOUGHT FOR TODAY

We are justified by Christ alone.

WISDOM FROM SCRIPTURE

We ourselves are Jews by birth and not Gentile sinners; yet we know that a person is justified not by the works of the law but through faith in Jesus Christ.

And we have come to believe in Christ Jesus, so that we might be justified by faith in Christ, and not by doing the works of the law, because no one will be justified by the works of the law.

But if, in our effort to be justified in Christ, we ourselves have been found to be sinners, is Christ then a servant of sin? Certainly not!

GALATIANS 2:15-17, NRSV

INSIGHTS FROM MARTIN LUTHER

Either we are not justified by Christ, or we are not justified by the law. The fact is, we are justified by Christ. Hence, we are not justified by the law. If we observe the law in order to be justified, or after having been justified by Christ we think we must further be justified by the law, we convert Christ into a legislator and a minister of sin.

"What are these false apostles doing?" Paul cries. "They are turning law into grace, and grace into law. They are changing Moses into Christ, and Christ into Moses. By teaching that besides Christ and his righteousness the performance of the law is necessary unto salvation, they put the law in the place of Christ; they attribute to the law the power to save, a power that belongs to Christ only." The proper office of Christ is to raise the sinner and extricate him from his sins.

Paul's argument has often comforted me. He argues: "If we who have been justified by Christ are counted unrighteous, why seek justification in Christ at all? If we are justified by the law, tell me, what has Christ achieved by his death, by his preaching, by his victory over sin and death? Either we are justified by Christ, or we are made worse sinners by him."

The sacred Scriptures, particularly those of the New Testament, make frequent mention of faith in Christ. "Whosoever believeth in him is saved, shall not perish, shall have everlasting life, is not judged." In open contradiction to the Scriptures, our opponents misquote, "He that believeth in Christ is condemned because he has faith without works." Our opponents turn everything topsy-turvy. They make Christ over into a murderer, and Moses into a saviour. Is not this horrible blasphemy?

The law requires perfect obedience. It condemns all who do not accomplish the will of God. But show me a person who is able to render perfect obedience. The law cannot justify. It can only condemn according to the passage: "Cursed is every one that continueth not in all things which are written in the book of the law to do them."

Paul has good reason for calling the minister of the law the minister of sin, for the law reveals our sinfulness. The realization of sin in turn frightens the heart and drives it to despair. Therefore, all exponents of the law and of works deserve to be called tyrants and oppressors.

The purpose of the law is to reveal sin. That this is the purpose of the law can be seen from the account of the giving of the law as reported in the nineteenth and twentieth chapters of Exodus. Moses brought the people out of their tents to have God speak to them personally from a cloud. But the people trembled with fear and fled. Standing aloof, they begged Moses, "Speak thou with us, and we will hear: but let not God speak with us, lest we die." The proper office of the law is to lead us out of our tents; in other words, out of the security of our self-trust and into the presence of God, that we may perceive his anger at our sinfulness.

All who say that faith alone in Christ does not justify a person, convert Christ into a minister of sin, a teacher of the law, and a cruel tyrant who requires the impossible. All merit-seekers take Christ for a new lawgiver.

In conclusion, if the law is the minister of sin, it is at the same time the minister of wrath and death. As the law reveals sin it fills a person with the fear of death and condemnation. Eventually the conscience wakes up to the fact that God is angry. If God is angry with you, he will destroy and condemn you forever. Unable to stand the thought of the wrath and judgment of God, many a person commits suicide.

The law drives us away from God, but Christ reconciles us to God, for "he is the Lamb of God, that taketh away the sins of the world." Now if the sin of the world is taken away, it is taken away from me. If sin is taken away, the wrath of God and his condemnation are also taken away. Let us practice this blessed conviction.

—*Commentary on the Epistle to the Galatians*

QUESTIONS TO CONSIDER

1. For you, what would be difficult about following the law?
2. How do you try to justify yourself?

A PRAYERFUL RESPONSE

Lord, I rely on you to justify me. Amen.

DAY 14

Crucified With Christ

THOUGHT FOR TODAY

We dare to live as though we are crucified with Christ.

WISDOM FROM SCRIPTURE

For through the law I died to the law, so that I might live to God. I have been crucified with Christ; and it is no longer I who live, but it is Christ who lives in me. And the life I now live in the flesh I live by faith in the Son of God, who loved me and gave himself for me.

I do not nullify the grace of God; for if justification comes through the law, then Christ died for nothing.

For all who rely on the works of the law are under a curse; for it is written, "Cursed is everyone who does not observe and obey all the things written in the book of the law."

Now it is evident that no one is justified before God by the law; for "The one who is righteous will live by faith."

But the law does not rest on faith; on the contrary, "Whoever does the works of the law will live by them."

Christ redeemed us from the curse of the law by becoming a curse for us—for it is written, "Cursed is everyone who hangs on a tree"—in order that in Christ Jesus the blessing of Abraham might come to the Gentiles, so that we might receive the promise of the Spirit through faith.

GALATIANS 2:19-21; 3:10-14, NRSV

Christ is Lord over the law because he was crucified unto the law. I also am lord over the law because by faith I am crucified with Christ. Paul does not here speak of crucifying the flesh, but he speaks of that higher crucifying wherein sin, the devil, and death are crucified in Christ and in me. By my faith in Christ I am crucified with Christ. Hence these evils are crucified and dead unto me.

"I do not mean to create the impression as though I did not live before this. But in reality I first live now, now that I have been delivered from the law, from sin, and death. Being crucified with Christ and dead unto the law, I may now rise unto a new and better life."

We must pay close attention to Paul's way of speaking. He says that we are crucified and dead unto the law. The fact is, the law is crucified and dead unto us. Paul purposely speaks that way in order to increase the portion of our comfort.

Paul explains what constitutes true Christian righteousness. True Christian righteousness is the righteousness of Christ who lives in us. We must look away from our own person. Christ and my conscience must become one, so that I can see nothing else but Christ crucified and raised from the dead for me. If I keep on looking at myself, I am gone.

If we lose sight of Christ and begin to consider our past, we simply go to pieces. We must turn our eyes to the brazen serpent, Christ crucified, and believe with all our hearts that he is our righteousness and our life. For Christ, on whom our eyes are fixed, in whom we live, who lives in us, is Lord over law, sin, death, and all evil.

"Thus, I live," the apostle starts out. But presently he corrects himself, saying, "Yet not I, but Christ liveth in me." He is the form of my perfection. He embellishes my faith.

Since Christ is now living in me, he abolishes the law, condemns sin, and destroys death in me. These foes vanish in his presence. Christ abiding in me drives out every evil. This union with Christ delivers me from the demands of the law and separates me from my sinful self. As long as I abide in Christ, nothing can hurt me.

When Christ makes his home in me, the old Adam has to stay outside and remain subject to the law. Think what grace, righteousness, life, peace, and salvation there is in me, thanks to that inseparable conjunction between Christ and me through faith!

Paul has a peculiar style, a celestial way of speaking. "I live," he says, "I live not; I am dead, I am not dead; I am a sinner, I am not a sinner; I have the law, I have no law." When we look at ourselves we find plenty of sin. But when we look at Christ, we have no sin. Whenever we separate the person of Christ from our own person, we live under the law and not in Christ; we are condemned by the law, dead before God.

Faith connects a person so intimately with Christ that he and the person he lives in become, as it were, one person. As such you may boldly say: "I am now one with Christ. Therefore Christ's righteousness, victory, and life are mine." On the other hand, Christ may say: "I am that big sinner. His sins and his death are mine, because he is joined to me and I to him."

Paul does not deny the fact that he is living in the flesh. He performs the natural functions of the flesh. But he says that this is not his real life. His life in the flesh is not a life after the flesh.

"I live by the faith of the Son of God," he says. "My speech is no longer directed by the flesh but by the Holy Spirit. My sight is no longer governed by the flesh but by the Holy Spirit. My hearing is no longer determined by the flesh but by the Holy Spirit. I cannot teach, write, pray, or give thanks without the instrumentality of the flesh; yet these activities do not proceed from the flesh, but from God."

A Christian uses earthly means like any unbeliever. Outwardly they look alike. Nevertheless, there is a great difference between them. I may live in the flesh, but I do not live after the flesh. I do my living now, "by the faith of the Son of God." Paul had the same voice, the same tongue, before and after his conversion. Before his conversion his tongue uttered blasphemies. But after his conversion his tongue spoke a spiritual, heavenly language.

We may now understand how spiritual life originates. It enters the heart by faith. Christ reigns in the heart with his Holy Spirit, who sees, hears, speaks, works, suffers, and does all things in and through us over the protest and the resistance of the flesh.

—*Commentary on the Epistle to the Galatians*

QUESTIONS TO CONSIDER
1. How does being "crucified with Christ" bring life?
2. What areas in your life need to be crucified with Christ?

A PRAYERFUL RESPONSE
Lord, reveal to me how I am to die to myself. Amen.

The Hope of Righteousness

THOUGHT FOR TODAY

Hope in what is not seen strengthens our faith.

WISDOM FROM SCRIPTURE

I consider that the sufferings of this present time are not worth comparing with the glory about to be revealed to us.

For the creation waits with eager longing for the revealing of the children of God; for the creation was subjected to futility, not of its own will but by the will of the one who subjected it, in hope that the creation itself will be set free from its bondage to decay and will obtain the freedom of the glory of the children of God.

We know that the whole creation has been groaning in labor pains until now; and not only the creation, but we ourselves, who have the first fruits of the Spirit, groan inwardly while we wait for adoption, the redemption of our bodies.

For in hope we were saved. Now hope that is seen is not hope. For who hopes for what is seen?

But if we hope for what we do not see, we wait for it with patience.

ROMANS 8:18-25, NRSV

INSIGHTS FROM MARTIN LUTHER

For we through the Spirit wait for the hope of righteousness by faith. Paul concludes the whole matter with this statement:

"You want to be justified by the law, by circumcision, and by works. We cannot see it. To be justified by such means would make Christ of no value to us. We would be obliged to perform the whole law. We rather through the Spirit wait for the hope of righteousness." The apostle is not satisfied to say "justified by faith." He adds hope to faith.

The Bible speaks of hope in two ways: as the object of the emotion and as the emotion itself. In the first chapter of the Epistle to the Colossians we have an instance of its first use: "For the hope which is laid up for you in heaven," in other words, the thing hoped for. In the sense of emotion we quote the passage from the eighth chapter of the Epistle to the Romans: "For we are saved by hope." As Paul uses the term "hope" here in writing to the Galatians, we may take it in either of its two meanings. We may understand Paul to say, "We wait in spirit, through faith, for the righteousness that we hope for, which in due time will be revealed to us." Or we may understand Paul to say, "We wait in Spirit by faith, for righteousness, with great hope and desire."

True, we are righteous, but our righteousness is not yet revealed; as long as we live here, sin stays with us. We cannot forget the law in our members striving against the law of our mind. When sin rages in our body and we through the Spirit wrestle against it, then we have cause for hope. We are not yet perfectly righteous. Perfect righteousness is still to be attained. Hence, we hope for it.

This is sweet comfort for us. And we are to make use of it in comforting the afflicted. We are to say to them: "Brother, you would like to feel God's favor as you feel your sin. But you are asking too much. Your righteousness rests on something much better than feelings. Wait and hope until it will be revealed to you in the Lord's own time. Don't go by your feelings, but go by the doctrine of faith, which pledges Christ to you."

The question occurs to us, What difference is there between faith and hope? We find it difficult to see any difference. Faith and hope are so closely linked that they cannot be separated. Still there is a difference between them.

First, hope and faith differ in regard to their sources. Faith originates in the understanding, while hope rises in the will.

Secondly, they differ in regard to their functions. Faith says what is to be done. Faith teaches, describes, directs. Hope exhorts the mind to be strong and courageous.

Thirdly, they differ in regard to their objectives. Faith concentrates on the truth. Hope looks to the goodness of God.

Fourthly, they differ in sequence. Faith is the beginning of life before tribulation. (See Hebrews 11.) Hope comes later and is born of tribulation. (See Romans 5.)

Finally, they differ in regard to their effects. Faith is a judge. It judges errors. Hope is a soldier. It fights against tribulations, the cross, despondency, despair, and waits for better things to come in the midst of evil.

Without hope, faith cannot endure. On the other hand, hope without faith is blind rashness and arrogance because it lacks knowledge. Before anything else a Christian must have the insight of faith, so that the intellect may know its directions in the day of trouble and the heart may hope for better things. By faith we begin; by hope we continue.

This passage contains excellent doctrine and much comfort. It declares that we are justified not by works, sacrifices, or ceremonies, but by Christ alone. The world may judge certain things to be ever so good; without Christ they are all wrong. Circumcision and the law and good works are carnal. "We," says Paul, "are above such things. We possess Christ by faith and in the midst of our afflictions we hopefully wait for the consummation of our righteousness."

You may say, "The trouble is, I don't feel as if I am righteous." You must not feel, but believe. Unless you believe that you are righteous, you do Christ a great wrong, for he has cleansed you by the washing of regeneration. He died for you so that through him you may obtain righteousness and everlasting life.

For in Jesus Christ neither circumcision availeth anything, nor uncircumcision, but faith which worketh by love. Faith must of course be sincere. It must be a faith that performs good works through love. If faith lacks love it is not true faith. Thus the apostle bars the way of hypocrites to the kingdom of Christ. He declares on the one hand, "In Christ Jesus circumcision availeth nothing." That is, works avail nothing. Faith alone, and that without any merit whatever, avails before God.

On the other hand, the apostle declares that without fruits faith serves no purpose. To think, "If faith justifies without works, let us work nothing," is to despise the grace of God. Idle faith is not justifying faith. In this terse manner Paul presents the whole life of a Christian. Inwardly it consists in faith towards God; outwardly it consists in love towards our fellowmen.

—*Commentary on the Epistle to the Galatians*

QUESTIONS TO CONSIDER

1. How does hope exhort us to be strong and courageous?
2. When do you need to rely most upon hope for strength?

A PRAYERFUL RESPONSE

Lord, thank you for hope to believe that what you promised will come to pass. Amen.

A Little Leaven

THOUGHT FOR TODAY

A "small" doctrinal error can eventually lead us astray.

WISDOM FROM SCRIPTURE

You were running well; who prevented you from obeying the truth?

Such persuasion does not come from the one who calls you.

A little yeast leavens the whole batch of dough.

I am confident about you in the Lord that you will not think otherwise. But whoever it is that is confusing you will pay the penalty.

But, my friends, why am I still being persecuted if I am still preaching circumcision? In that case the offense of the cross has been removed.

I wish those who unsettle you would castrate themselves!

For you were called to freedom, brothers and sisters; only do not use your freedom as an opportunity for self-indulgence, but through love become slaves to one another.

For the whole law is summed up in a single commandment, "You shall love your neighbor as yourself."

If, however, you bite and devour one another, take care that you are not consumed by one another.

GALATIANS 5:7-15, NRSV

Paul's concern for the Galatians meant nothing to some of them. Many had disowned him as their teacher and gone over to the false apostles. No doubt the false apostles took every occasion to defame Paul as a stubborn and contemptuous fellow who thought nothing of disrupting the unity of the churches for no other reason than his selfish pride and jealousy.

Other Galatians perhaps saw no harm in deviating a trifle from the doctrine of justification and faith. When they noticed that Paul made so much ado about a matter that seemed of no particular importance to them, they raised their eyebrows and thought within themselves: *What if we did deviate a little from the doctrine of Paul? What if we are a little to blame? He ought to overlook the whole matter and not make such an issue out of it, lest the unity of the churches be disturbed.* To this Paul replies: "A little leaven leaveneth the whole lump" (1 Corinthians 5:6).

Small faults grow into big faults. To tolerate a trifling error inevitably leads to crass heresy. The doctrine of the Bible is not ours to take or to allow liberties with. We have no right to change even a tittle of it. When it comes to life we are ready to do, to suffer, to forgive anything our opponents demand as long as faith and doctrine remain pure and uncorrupt. The apostle James says, "For whosoever shall keep the whole law and yet offend in one point, he is guilty of all" (James 2:10). This passage supports us over against our critics who claim that we disregard all charity to the great injury of the churches. We protest we desire nothing more than peace with all men. If they would only permit us to keep our doctrine of faith! The pure doctrine takes precedence before charity, apostles, or an angel from heaven.

Let others praise charity and unity to the skies; we magnify the authority of the Word and faith. Charity may be neglected at times without peril, but not the Word and faith. Charity suffers all things; it gives in. Faith suffers nothing; it never yields. Charity is often deceived but is never put out because it has nothing to lose; it continues to do well even to the ungrateful. When it comes to faith and salvation in the midst of lies and errors that parade as truth and deceive many, charity has no voice or vote. Let us not be influenced by the popular cry for charity and unity. If we do not love God and his Word, what difference does it make if we love anything at all? Paul, therefore, admonishes both teachers and hearers not to esteem lightly the doctrine of faith, as if it were a toy with which to amuse oneself in idle hours.

The question occurs to us whether Paul did well to trust the Galatians. Does not the Bible forbid us to trust in men? Faith trusts in God and is never wrong. Charity trusts in men and is often wrong. This charitable trust in man is necessary to life. Without it life would be impossible in the world. What kind of life would ours be if nobody could trust anybody else? True Christians are more ready to believe in men than the children of this world. Such charitable confidence is the fruit of the Spirit. Paul had such trust in the Galatians, although they had forsaken his doctrine. He trusted them "through the Lord," insofar as they were in Christ and Christ in them. Once they had forsaken Christ altogether, the apostle would trust the Galatians no longer.

The clause "whosoever he be" seems to indicate that the false apostles in outward appearance at least were very good and devout men. It may be that among them was some outstanding disciple of the apostles, a man of fame and authority. The apostle Paul must have been faced by this very situation, otherwise his vehemence would have been uncalled for. No doubt many of the Galatians were taken aback with the vehemency of the apostle. They perhaps thought: Why should he be so stubborn in such small matters? Why is he so quick to pronounce damnation upon his brethren in the ministry?

I cannot say it often enough that we must carefully differentiate between doctrine and life. Doctrine is a piece of heaven; life is a piece of earth. Life is sin, error, uncleanness, misery, in which charity must forbear, believe, hope, and suffer all things. Forgiveness of sins must be continuous so that sin and error may not be defended and sustained. But with doctrine there must be no error, no need of pardon. There can be no comparison between doctrine and life. The least little point of doctrine is of greater importance than heaven and earth. Therefore, we cannot allow the least jot of doctrine to be corrupted.

Jesus held out the same comfort to his disciples in the fifth chapter of Matthew. "Blessed are ye, when men shall revile you and persecute you, and shall say all manner of evil against you falsely, for my sake. Rejoice, and be exceeding glad; for great is your reward in heaven" (Matthew 5:11-12). The Church must not come short of this joy.

Briefly, as long as the Church proclaims the doctrine, she must suffer persecution because the gospel declares the mercy and glory of God. This in turn stirs up the devil because the gospel shows him up for what he is, the devil, and not God. Therefore, as long as the gospel holds sway, persecution plays the accompaniment, or else there is something the matter with the devil. When he is hit, you will know it by the havoc he raises everywhere.

—*Commentary on the Epistle to the Galatians*

QUESTIONS TO CONSIDER
1. Why is biblical doctrine important?
2. How do you feel about Luther's stand on doctrine?

A PRAYERFUL RESPONSE
Lord, teach me the truth revealed in your Word. Amen.

Walk in the Spirit

THOUGHT FOR TODAY
Our flesh must be led by the Holy Spirit.

WISDOM FROM SCRIPTURE
Live by the Spirit, I say, and do not gratify the desires of the flesh.

For what the flesh desires is opposed to the Spirit, and what the Spirit desires is opposed to the flesh; for these are opposed to each other, to prevent you from doing what you want.

But if you are led by the Spirit, you are not subject to the law.

Now the works of the flesh are obvious: fornication, impurity, licentiousness, idolatry, sorcery, enmities, strife, jealousy, anger, quarrels, dissensions, factions, envy, drunkenness, carousing, and things like these. I am warning you, as I warned you before: those who do such things will not inherit the kingdom of God.

By contrast, the fruit of the Spirit is love, joy, peace, patience, kindness, generosity, faithfulness, gentleness, and self-control. There is no law against such things.

And those who belong to Christ Jesus have crucified the flesh with its passions and desires.

If we live by the Spirit, let us also be guided by the Spirit.

Let us not become conceited, competing against one another, envying one another.

GALATIANS 5:16-26, NRSV

"I have not forgotten what I told you about faith in the first part of my letter. Because I exhort you to mutual love you are not to think that I have gone back on my teaching of justification by faith alone. I am still of the same opinion. To remove every possibility for misunderstanding I have added this explanatory note: 'Walk in the Spirit, and ye shall not fulfill the lust of the flesh.'"

With this verse Paul explains how he wants this sentence to be understood: "By love serve one another. When I bid you to love one another, this is what I mean and require, 'Walk in the Spirit.' I know very well you will not fulfill the law, because you are sinners as long as you live. Nevertheless, you should endeavor to walk in the Spirit, that is, fight against the flesh and follow the leading of the Holy Spirit."

It is quite apparent that Paul had not forgotten the doctrine of justification, for in bidding the Galatians to walk in the Spirit, he at the same time denies that good works can justify. "When I speak of the fulfilling of the law I do not mean to say that you are justified by the law. All I mean to say is that you should take the Spirit for your guide and resist the flesh. That is the most you shall ever be able to do. Obey the Spirit and fight against the flesh."

The lust of the flesh is not altogether extinct in us. It rises up again and again and wrestles with the Spirit. No flesh, not even that of the true believer, is so completely under the influence of the Spirit that it will not bite or devour, or at least neglect, the commandment of love. At the slightest provocation it flares up, demands to be revenged, and hates a neighbor like an enemy, or at least does not love him as much as he ought to be loved.

Therefore Paul establishes this rule of love for the believers. Serve one another in love. Bear the infirmities of your brother. Forgive one another. Without such bearing and forbearing, giving and forgiving, there can be no unity because to give and to take offense are unavoidably human.

Whenever you are angry with your brother for any cause, repress your violent emotions through the Spirit. Bear with his weakness and love him. He does not cease to be your neighbor or brother because he offended you. On the contrary, he now more than ever before requires your loving attention.

The scholastics take the lust of the flesh to mean carnal lust. True, believers too are tempted with carnal lust. Even the married are not immune to carnal lusts. Men set little value upon that which they have and covet what they have not, as the poet says: "The things most forbidden we always desire, And things most denied we seek to acquire."

I do not deny that the lust of the flesh includes carnal lust. But it takes in more. It takes in all the corrupt desires with which the believers are more or less infected, such as pride, hatred, covetousness, impatience. Later on Paul enumerates even idolatry and heresy among the works of the flesh. The apostle's meaning is clear. "I want you to love one another. But you do not do it. In fact, because of your flesh, you cannot do it." Hence we cannot be justified by deeds of love.

Do not for a moment think that I am reversing myself on my stand concerning faith. Faith and hope must continue. By faith we are justified; by hope we endure to the end. In addition we serve each other in love because true faith is not idle. Our love, however, is faulty. In bidding you to walk in the

Spirit I indicate to you that our love is not sufficient to justify us. Neither do I demand that you should get rid of the flesh, but that you should control and subdue it.

When Paul declares that "the flesh lusteth against the Spirit, and the Spirit against the flesh," he means to say that we are not to think, speak, or do the things to which the flesh incites us. He knows that the flesh courts sin. The thing for us to do is to resist the flesh by the Spirit. But if we abandon the leadership of the Spirit for that of the flesh, we are going to fulfill the lust of the flesh and die in our sins.

—*Commentary on the Epistle to the Galatians*

QUESTIONS TO CONSIDER

1. What fleshly desires do you struggle with?
2. How can your fleshly desires be controlled by the Spirit?

A PRAYERFUL RESPONSE

Lord, I surrender my desires to your control. Amen.

Temptation and Tribulation

THOUGHT FOR TODAY

Through our temptation and tribulation we identify with Christ.

WISDOM FROM SCRIPTURE

But we have this treasure in clay jars, so that it may be made clear that this extraordinary power belongs to God and does not come from us.

We are afflicted in every way, but not crushed; perplexed, but not driven to despair; persecuted, but not forsaken; struck down, but not destroyed; always carrying in the body the death of Jesus, so that the life of Jesus may also be made visible in our bodies.

For while we live, we are always being given up to death for Jesus' sake, so that the life of Jesus may be made visible in our mortal flesh.

So death is at work in us, but life in you.

But just as we have the same spirit of faith that is in accordance with scripture—"I believed, and so I spoke"—we also believe, and so we speak, because we know that the one who raised the Lord Jesus will raise us also with Jesus, and will bring us with you into his presence.

Yes, everything is for your sake, so that grace, as it extends to more and more people, may increase thanksgiving, to the glory of God.

So we do not lose heart. Even though our outer nature is wasting away, our inner nature is being renewed day by day.

For this slight momentary affliction is preparing us for an eternal weight of glory beyond all measure, because we look not at what can be seen but at what cannot be seen; for what can be seen is temporary, but what cannot be seen is eternal.

2 CORINTHIANS 4:7-19, NRSV

INSIGHTS FROM MARTIN LUTHER

Whoever, without the word of grace and prayer, disputes with the devil about sin and the law will lose. For the devil is armed against us with Goliath's sword, with his spear and weapons; he has on his side the testimony of our own consciences, which witness against us that we have transgressed all God's commandments. Therefore, the devil has a very great advantage against us.

The devil often assaults me by objecting that out of my doctrine great offenses and much evil have proceeded, and with this he many a time vehemently perplexes me. Although I tell him that much good is also raised thereby, which by God's grace is true, yet he is so nimble a spirit, and so crafty a rhetorician, that, master-like, he can pervert this into sin. He was never so fierce and full of rage as he is now. I feel him well.

But when I remember myself, and take hold on the gospel, and meet him with the Word, then I overcome him and refute all his arguments; yet for a time I often fail. He tells me the law is also God's Word; why, then, is the gospel always objected against me?

I reply that the law is also God's Word, but it is as far different from the gospel as heaven from earth; for in the gospel,

God offers to us his grace. He will be our God merely out of love, and he presents to us his only begotten Son, who delivers us from sin and death and has purchased for us everlasting righteousness and life. I hold on to this truth. God has indeed also given the law, but in every respect for another use and purpose.

What I teach and preach, I teach openly, by clear daylight, not in a corner. I direct the same by the gospel, by baptism, and by the Lord's prayer. Here Christ stands; him I cannot deny; upon the gospel do I ground my cause. Yet the devil, with his crafty disputing, brings it so near unto me that the sweat of anguish drops from me.

Therefore, be of good courage and think from now on that you are not the child of a human creature, but of God, through faith in Christ, in whose name you are baptized. Therefore, the spear of death cannot enter into you; the devil has no right unto you, much less can he hurt or prejudice you, for he is everlastingly swallowed up through Christ.

It is better for a Christian to be sorrowful than secure, as the people of this world are. Well is it for him that stands always in fear, yet knows he has in heaven a gracious God, for Christ's sake.

There are two sorts of tribulations; one of the spirit; another of the flesh. Satan torments the conscience with lies, perverting that which is done uprightly and according to God's Word; but the body or flesh he plagues in another kind.

If Satan had not so plagued and exercised me, I should not have been so great an enemy unto him or have been able to do him such hurt. Tribulation keeps us from pride, and therewith increases the acknowledgment of Christ and of God's gifts and benefits. For, from the time I began to be in tribulation, God gave me the victory of overcoming that confounded, cursed, and blasphemous life wherein I lived. God did the business in such a way that neither the emperor nor the pope was able to suppress me, but the devil must come and set upon me so that God's strength may be known in my weakness.

Our tribulations and doubts, by which the devil plagues us, can be driven away by no better means than by condemning him, as when one condemns a fierce cur. In passing quietly by, the dog then not only desists from biting, but also from barking. But when one enrages him by timorously throwing something at him, then he falls upon the person and bites him. Even so, when the devil sees that we fear him, he continually torments and plagues us.

When Satan will not leave off tempting you, then bear with patience. Hold on, hand and foot. Do not faint, as if there would be no end thereof. Stand courageously, and attend God's leisure, knowing that what the devil cannot accomplish by his sudden and powerful assaults he thinks to gain by craft, by persevering to vex and tempt you, thereby to make you faint and weary. Be fully assured that in this sport with the devil, God, with all his holy angels, takes delight and joy; and assure yourself, also, that the end thereof will be blessed and happy, which you shall certainly find to your everlasting comfort.

We can find no instance of any human creature oppressed with such sorrow as to sweat blood. Therefore, this history of Christ is wonderful; no man can understand or conceive what his bloody sweat is. And it is more wonderful that the Lord of grace and of wrath, of life and of death, should be so weak and made so sorrowful as to be constrained to seek for solace and comfort of poor and miserable sinners, and to say: Ah, loving disciples! sleep not, wake yet a little, and talk one with another, that at least I may hear some people are about me.

"We see Jesus, who was made a little lower than the angels for the suffering of death" (Hebrews 2:9). Ah, Saviour Christ Jesus, through the immeasurable heavy burden which lay on his innocent back; namely, the sins of the whole world.

—Of Temptation and Tribulation

QUESTIONS TO CONSIDER
1. What has been your greatest tribulation?
2. How did God help you through?

A PRAYERFUL RESPONSE
Lord, thank you for using temptation and tribulation to purify me. Amen.

The Devil and His Works

THOUGHT FOR TODAY

The devil is our one true enemy.

WISDOM FROM SCRIPTURE

I exhort the elders among you to tend the flock of God that is in your charge, exercising the oversight, not under compulsion but willingly, as God would have you do it—not for sordid gain but eagerly.

Do not lord it over those in your charge, but be examples to the flock.

And when the chief shepherd appears, you will win the crown of glory that never fades away.

In the same way, you who are younger must accept the authority of the elders. And all of you must clothe yourselves with humility in your dealings with one another, for "God opposes the proud, but gives grace to the humble."

Humble yourselves therefore under the mighty hand of God, so that he may exalt you in due time.

Cast all your anxiety on him, because he cares for you.

Discipline yourselves, keep alert. Like a roaring lion your adversary the devil prowls around, looking for someone to devour.

Resist him, steadfast in your faith, for you know that your brothers and sisters in all the world are undergoing the same kinds of suffering.

And after you have suffered for a little while, the God of all grace, who has called you to his eternal glory in Christ, will himself restore, support, strengthen, and establish you.

1 PETER 5:2-10, NRSV

INSIGHTS FROM MARTIN LUTHER

When I was young, someone told me this story: Satan had, in vain, set all his craft and subtlety at work to separate a married pair that lived together in perfect harmony and love. At last, having concealed a razor under each of their pillows, he visited the husband, disguised as an old woman, and told him that his wife had plotted to kill him. He next told the same thing to the wife. The husband, finding the razor under his wife's pillow, became furious with anger at her supposed wickedness and cut her throat. So powerful is Satan in his malice.

The devil seduces us at first by all the allurements of sin in order to plunge us into despair; he pampers up the flesh, that he may, by and by, prostrate the spirit. We feel no pain in the act of sin, but afterwards the soul is sad and the conscience disturbed.

He who has, for his master and king, Jesus Christ, the son of the Virgin, who took upon himself our flesh and our blood, will have the devil for his enemy. The devil cannot but be our enemy, since we war against him with God's Word, and with it we destroy his kingdom. He is a prince and god of the world and has a greater power than all the kings, potentates, and princes upon earth. This is why he wants revenge on us and assaults us without ceasing. But we have a great advantage against the devil. As powerful, wicked, and cunning as he is, he cannot hurt us, since it is not against him we have sinned, but against God. Therefore we have nothing to do with that arch-enemy; but we confess: "Against thee, Lord, have we sinned."

We know that we have a gracious God and a merciful Father in heaven, whose wrath against us Christ Jesus, our only Lord and Saviour, has appeased with his precious blood. Now, just as through Christ we have remission of sins and peace with God, so must the envious devil be content to let us alone, in peace, so that he can neither upbraid nor hit us in the teeth concerning our sins against God's laws. For Christ has canceled and torn in pieces the handwriting of our consciences, which was a witness against us, and nailed the same to his cross. To God be everlasting honor, praise, and glory in Christ Jesus. Amen.

The devil knows the thoughts of the ungodly, for he inspires them. He sees and rules the hearts of all people who are not kept safe and preserved by God's Word; yea, he holds them captive in his snares, so that they must think, do, and speak according to his will. As Paul says: "The god of this world has blinded the minds of the unbelievers, to keep them from seeing the light of the gospel of the glory of Christ, who is the image of God" (2 Corinthians 4:4, NRSV). And Christ gives a reason how it comes to pass that many hear the Word yet neither understand nor keep the same, where he says: "The evil one comes and snatches away what is sown in the heart; this is what was sown on the path" (Matthew 13:19, NRSV). Therefore, it is no marvel that the devil, through his prophets, declares what shall happen and come to pass.

The Scriptures clearly show that the devil gives unto mankind evil thoughts and suggests evil projects to the ungodly. Of Judas it is written that the devil put it into his heart to betray Christ. And he not only instigated Cain to hate his brother Abel, but to murder him.

However, the devil knows not the thoughts of the righteous until they utter them. He knew not the thoughts of Christ's heart, nor does he know the thoughts of the godly, in whose heart Christ dwells. The devil is a powerful, crafty, and subtle spirit. Christ names him the Prince of the World. He goes about shooting his fiery darts into the hearts of people, even the hearts of the godly, as discord, hatred to God, despair, blaspheming. Paul well understood all these assaults and bitterly complained of them.

The apostle Paul gives this title to the devil: "That he hath the power of death." And Christ calls him a murderer. He is so skilled that he is able to cause death even with the leaf of a tree. He has more boxes and pots full of poisons, with which he destroys men, than all the apothecaries in the world have of healing medicine. If one poison will not dispatch, another will. In a word, the power of the devil is greater than we can imagine; it is only God's finger that can resist him.

When tribulations approach, excommunicate them in the name of Christ Jesus, and say: God has forbidden me to receive that coin, because it is minted by the devil; we reject it as prohibited. When heavy temptations come upon you, expel them by what means you have; talk with good friends about such things as you take delight in.

The devil gives heaven to people before they sin, but after they sin, brings their consciences into despair. Christ deals in the opposite way; for he gives heaven after sins are committed and makes consciences joyful.

—Of the Devil and His Works

QUESTIONS TO CONSIDER

1. In what ways does Satan attack you?
2. How do you do spiritual battle against your enemy?

A PRAYERFUL RESPONSE

Lord, with your help I will win the spiritual battles I face today. Amen.

DAY 20

The Way of Idolatry

THOUGHT FOR TODAY

We are called to worship the one true God.

WISDOM FROM SCRIPTURE

Therefore, my dear friends, flee from the worship of idols.

I speak as to sensible people; judge for yourselves what I say.

The cup of blessing that we bless, is it not a sharing in the blood of Christ? The bread that we break, is it not a sharing in the body of Christ?

Because there is one bread, we who are many are one body, for we all partake of the one bread.

Consider the people of Israel; are not those who eat the sacrifices partners in the altar?

What do I imply then? That food sacrificed to idols is anything, or that an idol is anything?

No, I imply that what pagans sacrifice, they sacrifice to demons and not to God. I do not want you to be partners with demons.

You cannot drink the cup of the Lord and the cup of demons. You cannot partake of the table of the Lord and the table of demons.

1 CORINTHIANS 10:14-21, NRSV

All manner of religion, where people serve God without his Word and command, is simply idolatry. The more holy and spiritual such a religion seems, the more hurtful and venomous it is, for it leads people away from the faith of Christ and makes them rely and depend upon their own strength, works, and righteousness.

When I was asked that if a man, out of good intention, should erect a pious work without God's Word or command, does he serve a true or a strange God, I answered that if a man honors God and calls upon him to the end he may expect comfort, help, and all good from him. Now, if this same honor and calling upon God be done according to God's Word—that is, when a man expects from him all graces for the sake of his promises made unto us in Christ—then he honors the true, living, and everlasting God. But if a man takes in hand a work or a service out of his own devotion, as he thinks good, thereby to appease God's anger or to obtain forgiveness of sins, everlasting life, and salvation, as is the manner of all hypocrites and seeming holy workers, then, I say flatly, he honors and worships an idol in heart and it helps him nothing at all that he thinks he does it to the honor of the true God. For that which is not faith is sin.

Hypocrites and idolaters are of the same quality with singers who will scarce sing when asked to do so, but when not desired, begin and never leave off. Even so with the false workers of holiness; when God orders them to obey his commands, which are to love one's neighbor, to help him with advice, with lending, giving, admonishing, and comforting, no man can bring them to this. On the contrary, they stick to that which they themselves choose to do, pretending that this is the best way to honor and serve God—a great delusion of theirs. They plague and torment their bodies with fasting, praying, singing, reading; they affect great humility and holiness, and do all things with vast zeal, fervency, and incessant devotion. But such as the service and work is, such will also the reward be, as Christ himself says: "In vain do they worship me, teaching for doctrine the commandments of men."

Paul talks about serving God without knowing him. That is, when as yet you knew not God or what God's will was towards you, you served those who by nature were not gods; you served the dreams and thoughts of your hearts. Against God's Word you constructed a God who suffered himself to be conciliated with such works and worshiping as your devotion and good intention chose. For all idolatry in the world arises from this, that people by nature have had the common knowledge that there is a God, without which idolatry would remain unpracticed. With this knowledge engrafted in mankind, they have, without consulting God's Word, fancied all manner of ungodly opinions of God, and held and esteemed these for divine truths, imagining a God otherwise than, by nature, he is.

All these sins, preachers ought boldly and freely to reprove, not regarding men's high dignities and powers. For the prophets, as we see in Hosea, reproved and threatened not only the house of Israel in general, but also, in particular, the priests, aye, the king himself, and the whole court. They cared not for the great danger that might follow from the magistrate being so openly assailed, or that they should fall into displeasure or contempt and their preaching be esteemed rebellious. They were impelled by a far greater danger, lest by such examples of the higher powers the subjects also should be seduced into sin.

But thus goes the world; superstition, unbelief, false doctrine, and idolatry obtain more credit and profit than the upright, true, and pure religion.

God and God's worship are relatives; the one cannot be without the other, for God must always be the God of some people or nation. God will have some to call upon him and honor him; for to have a God and to honor him go together. Therefore, whoever brings in a divine worship of his own selection, without God's command, is an adulterer, like a married woman who consents to another man, seeking another and not the upright true God. It avails him nothing that he thinks he does God service herein.

—Of Idolatry

QUESTIONS TO CONSIDER

1. Do you have any "idols" in your life?
2. If so, why do you hold on to them?

A PRAYERFUL RESPONSE

Lord, help me to see that you alone are to be worshiped. Amen.

DAY 21

The Way of the World

THOUGHT FOR TODAY

The world offers nothing lasting to us.

WISDOM FROM SCRIPTURE

For the wise man, like the fool, will not be long remembered; in days to come both will be forgotten. Like the fool, the wise man too must die!

So I hated life, because the work that is done under the sun was grievous to me. All of it is meaningless, a chasing after the wind.

I hated all the things I had toiled for under the sun, because I must leave them to the one who comes after me.

And who knows whether he will be a wise man or a fool? Yet he will have control over all the work into which I have poured my effort and skill under the sun. This too is meaningless.

So my heart began to despair over all my toilsome labor under the sun.

For a man may do his work with wisdom, knowledge and skill, and then he must leave all he owns to someone who has not worked for it. This too is meaningless and a great misfortune.

What does a man get for all the toil and anxious striving with which he labors under the sun?

All his days his work is pain and grief; even at night his mind does not rest. This too is meaningless.

A man can do nothing better than to eat and drink and find satisfaction in his work. This too, I see, is from the hand of God, for without him, who can eat or find enjoyment?

To the man who pleases him, God gives wisdom, knowledge and happiness, but to the sinner he gives the task of gathering and storing up wealth to hand it over to the one who pleases God. This too is meaningless, a chasing after the wind.

ECCLESIASTES 2:16-26, NIV

INSIGHTS FROM MARTIN LUTHER

He that is now a prince, wants to be a king or an emperor.

A man in love with a girl is ever casting about how he may come to marry her, and in his eyes there is none fairer than she. When he has got her, he is soon weary of her and thinks another more fair, whom easily he might have had.

The poor man thinks, had I but twenty pounds I should be rich enough; but when he has got that, he would have more. The heart is inconsistent in all things.

The wickedness of the enemies of the Word is not human, but altogether devilish. A human creature is wicked according to the manner and nature of mankind, and according as he is spoiled through original sin. But when he is possessed and driven of the devil, then begins the most bitter and cruel combat between him and the woman's seed.

The world will neither hold God for God, nor the devil for the devil. And if a man were left to himself, to do after his own kind and nature, he would willingly throw our Lord God out the window; for the world has no regard for God. As the psalm says: "The wicked man saith in his heart, there is no God."

The god of the world is riches, pleasure, and pride, by which it abuses all the creatures and gifts of God. We have the nature and manner of all wild beasts in eating. The wolves eat sheep; we also. The foxes eat hens and geese; we also. The hawks and kites eat fowl and birds; we also. Pikes eat other fish; we also. With oxen, horses, and kine, we also eat salads and grass.

I much wonder how the heathen could write such fair and excellent things about death, seeing it is so grisly and fearful! But when I remember the nature of the world, then I wonder nothing at all; for they saw great evil and wickedness flourishing among them and in their rulers, which sorely grieved them, and they had nothing else to threaten and terrify their rulers with but death.

Now, if the heathen so little regarded death, nay, so highly and honorably esteemed it, how much more so ought we Christians? For they, poor people, knew less than nothing of life eternal, while we know and are instructed in it. Yet, when we only speak of death, we are all afraid.

The cause is our sins; we live worse than the heathen, and therefore cannot justly complain, for the greater our sins the more fearful is death. See those who have rejected God's Word; when they are at the point of death and are put in mind of the day of judgment, how fearfully do they tremble and shake.

There are three sorts of people: the first, the common sort, who live secure without remorse of conscience, without acknowledging their corrupt manners and natures, insensible of God's wrath against their sins, and careless about how they live. The second, those who through the law are scared, feel God's anger, and strive and wrestle with despair. The third, those who acknowledge their sins and God's merited wrath, feel themselves conceived and born in sin, and therefore deserving of condemnation. However, they attentively hearken to the gospel and believe that God, out of grace, for the sake of Jesus Christ, forgives sins. They are justified before God and afterwards show the fruits of their faith by all manner of good works.

The heart of a human creature is like quicksilver, now here, now there; this day so, tomorrow otherwise. Therefore, vanity is a poor miserable thing, as Ecclesiastes says. A man desires and longs after things that are uncertain and of doubtful result, but condemns that which is certain, done, and accomplished. Therefore, what God gives us we will not have; for this reason Christ would not govern on earth, but gave it over to the devil, saying, "Rule thou." God is of another nature, manner, and mind. "I," he says, "am God, and therefore change not; I hold fast and keep sure my promises and threatenings."

The highest wisdom of the world is to busy itself with temporal, earthly, and ephemeral things; and when these go ill, it says, "Who would have thought it?" But faith is a certain and sure expectation of that which a man hopes for, making no doubt of that which yet he sees not. A true Christian is most certain that the beloved cross is near at hand; and thus he is not afraid when it goes ill with him and he is tormented. But the world, and those who live secure in it, cannot bear misfortune; they go on continually, dancing in pleasure and delight, like the rich glutton in the gospel.

—The Nature of the World

QUESTIONS TO CONSIDER

1. If the world is so fruitless, why are we drawn to it?
2. How can you learn to discern the temporal from the eternal?

A PRAYERFUL RESPONSE

Lord, teach me to desire more of your heavenly kingdom. Amen.

DAY 22

On Vocation and Calling

THOUGHT FOR TODAY

We need to follow God's timing for our calling.

WISDOM FROM SCRIPTURE

We ought always to thank God for you, brothers, and rightly so, because your faith is growing more and more, and the love every one of you has for each other is increasing.

Therefore, among God's churches we boast about your perseverance and faith in all the persecutions and trials you are enduring.

All this is evidence that God's judgment is right, and as a result you will be counted worthy of the kingdom of God, for which you are suffering.

God is just: He will pay back trouble to those who trouble you and give relief to you who are troubled, and to us as well. This will happen when the Lord Jesus is revealed from heaven in blazing fire with his powerful angels.

He will punish those who do not know God and do not obey the gospel of our Lord Jesus.

They will be punished with everlasting destruction and shut out from the presence of the Lord and from the majesty of his power on the day he comes to be glorified in his holy people and to be marveled at among all those who have believed. This includes you, because you believed our testimony to you.

With this in mind, we constantly pray for you, that our God

may count you worthy of his calling, and that by his power he may fulfill every good purpose of yours and every act prompted by your faith.

We pray this so that the name of our Lord Jesus may be glorified in you, and you in him, according to the grace of our God and the Lord Jesus Christ.

2 THESSALONIANS 1:3-12, NIV

INSIGHTS FROM MARTIN LUTHER

When they who have the office of teaching do not take joy in it, that is, have no regard to him that called and sent them, it is, for them, an irksome work.

It is much to be lamented that no man is content and satisfied with that which God gives him in his vocation and calling. As the heathen have said, Other men's conditions please us more than our own. And another heathen statement: The more we have the more we want. To serve God is for everyone to remain in his vocation and calling, be it ever so mean and simple.

It is said that occasion has a forelock but is bald behind. Our Lord has taught this by the course of nature. A farmer must sow his barley and oats about Easter; if he defer it to Michaelmas [September 29], it were too late. When apples are ripe they must be plucked from the tree or they are spoiled. Procrastination is as bad as overhastiness. There is my servant Wolf: When four or five birds fall upon the bird net, he will not draw it, but says: Oh, I will wait until more come; then they all fly away and he gets none.

Regarding calling, occasion is a great matter. Terence says well: I came in time, which is the chief thing of all. Julius Caesar understood occasion; Pompey and Hannibal did not. Boys at school understand it not, therefore they must have fathers and masters with the rod to hold them so that they neglect not time and lose it. Many a young fellow has a school stipend for six or seven years, during which he ought diligently to study; he has his tutors, and other means, but he thinks: Oh, I have time enough yet. But I say: No, fellow. What little Jack learns not, great John learns not. Occasion salutes you, and reaches out her forelock to you, saying: "Here I am, take hold of me"; you think she will come again. Then says she: "Well, seeing you will not take hold of my top, take hold of my tail"; and then she flings away.

Bonaventura was but a poor sophist, yet he could say: He that neglects occasion is of it neglected. And it is a saying with us: Take hold of time, while 'tis time, and now, while 'tis now.

—Of Vocation and Calling

QUESTIONS TO CONSIDER

1. What is your calling from God?
2. If you are not sure of your calling, how might you discover it?

A PRAYERFUL RESPONSE

Lord, I will follow your timing for the calling you have given to me. Amen.

PART THREE

Praying by Petition

Our Father, thou in heaven above,
Who biddest us to dwell in love,
As brethren of one family,
To cry in every need to thee,
Teach us no thoughtless word to say,
But from our inmost heart to pray.

Amen, that is, So shall it be.
Confirm our faith and hope in thee
That we may doubt not, but believe
What here we ask we shall receive.
Thus in thy name and at thy word
We say: Amen. Oh, hear us, Lord! Amen.

From "Our Father, Thou in Heaven Above"
by Martin Luther

MARTIN LUTHER'S INSIGHT
God's work is accomplished through prayer.

DAY 23

Called to Prayer

THOUGHT FOR TODAY
We are called to prayer, just as we are.

WISDOM FROM SCRIPTURE
"And when you pray, do not be like the hypocrites, for they love to pray standing in the synagogues and on the street corners to be seen by men. I tell you the truth, they have received their reward in full.

"But when you pray, go into your room, close the door and pray to your Father, who is unseen. Then your Father, who sees what is done in secret, will reward you."

MATTHEW 6:5-6, NIV

Is any one of you in trouble? He should pray. Is anyone happy? Let him sing songs of praise.

Is any one of you sick? He should call the elders of the church to pray over him and anoint him with oil in the name of the Lord.

And the prayer offered in faith will make the sick person well; the Lord will raise him up. If he has sinned, he will be forgiven.

Therefore confess your sins to each other and pray for each other so that you may be healed. The prayer of a righteous man is powerful and effective.

Elijah was a man just like us. He prayed earnestly that it

would not rain, and it did not rain on the land for three and a half years.

Again he prayed, and the heavens gave rain, and the earth produced its crops.

JAMES 5:13-18, NIV

INSIGHTS FROM MARTIN LUTHER

No one should by any means despise his prayer, but rather set great store by it, and realize it is as important to obey the command to pray as to obey any other of the Lord's commands. A child should by no means despise his obedience to father and mother, but should always think: This work is a work of obedience, and what I do, I do with no other intention than that I may walk in the obedience and commandment of God, on which I can stand firm and esteem it a great thing, not on account of my worthiness, but on account of the commandment.

So here also, for what we pray we should regard as demanded by God and done in obedience to him, and should reflect thus: On my account it would amount to nothing; but it shall avail, for the reason that God has commanded it. Everybody, no matter what he has to say in prayer, should always come before God in obedience to this commandment.

We pray, therefore, and exhort everyone most diligently to take this to heart and by no means to despise his prayer. In times past it has been taught that no one regarded these things, and men supposed it to be sufficient to have done the work, whether God would hear it or not. But that is staking prayer on a risk, and murmuring it at a venture, and therefore it is a lost prayer. Such thoughts as these lead us astray and deter us:

I am not holy or worthy enough; if I were as godly and holy as Peter or Paul, then I would pray. Put such thoughts far away, for just the same commandment which applied to Paul applies also to us.

Therefore, you should say: My prayer is as precious, holy, and pleasing to God as that of Paul or of the most holy saints. I will gladly grant that Paul is holier in his person, but not on account of the commandment, since God does not regard prayer on account of the person but on account of his Word and obedience to it. For on the commandment on which all the saints rest their prayer I, too, rest mine. Moreover I pray for the same thing for which they all pray and ever have prayed; besides, I have just as great a need of it as those great saints, yea, even a greater one than they.

Let this be the first and most important point, that all our prayers must be based and rest upon obedience to God, irrespective of our person, whether we be sinners or saints, worthy or unworthy. And we must know that God will not have it treated as a jest, but be angry, and punish all who do not pray, as surely as he punishes all other disobedience. Next, that he will not suffer our prayers to be in vain or lost. For if he did not intend to answer your prayer, he would not bid you to pray.

In the second place, we should feel urged and incited to pray because God has also added a promise and declared that it shall surely be done to us as we pray, as he says in Psalm 50:15: "Call upon Me in the day of trouble: I will deliver thee." And Christ in the Gospel of Matthew 7:7: "Ask, and it shall be given you. For every one that asketh receiveth." Such promises ought to encourage and kindle our hearts to pray with pleasure and delight, since God testifies with his [own] Word that our prayer is heartily pleasing to him, moreover, that it shall assuredly be heard and granted in order that we may not despise it or think lightly of it.

This you can hold up to him and say: Here I come, dear Father, and pray not of my own purpose nor upon my own worthiness but at thy commandment and promise, which cannot fail or deceive me. Whoever, therefore, does not believe this promise must know again that he excites God to anger as a person who most highly dishonors him and reproaches him with falsehood.

Besides this, we should be incited and drawn to prayer because in addition to this commandment and promise, God anticipates us and himself arranges the words and form of prayer for us, and places them upon our lips as to how and what we should pray, that we may see how heartily he pities us in our distress and may never doubt that such prayer is pleasing to him and shall certainly be answered. [The Lord's Prayer] is a great advantage indeed over all other prayers that we might compose. For in them the conscience would ever be in doubt and say: I have prayed, but who knows how it pleases him, or whether I have hit upon the right proportions and form? Hence there is no nobler prayer to be found upon earth than the Lord's Prayer, which we daily pray because it has this excellent testimony, that God loves to hear it, which we ought not to surrender for all the riches of the world.

And it has been prescribed also that we should see and consider the distress which ought to urge and compel us to pray without ceasing. For whoever would pray must have something to present, state, and name which he desires; if not, it cannot be called a prayer.

—*Of Prayer, The Large Catechism*

QUESTIONS TO CONSIDER

1. What barriers interfere with your prayer time?
2. How can you surrender those things to God during prayer?

A PRAYERFUL RESPONSE

Lord, remind me that you desire a relationship with me through prayer. Amen.

DAY 24

The Earnest Prayer

THOUGHT FOR TODAY
Earnest prayer opens our hearts to receive from God.

WISDOM FROM SCRIPTURE
"And when you pray, do not keep on babbling like pagans, for they think they will be heard because of their many words.

"Do not be like them, for your Father knows what you need before you ask him."

MATTHEW 6:7-8, NIV

Finally, be strong in the Lord and in his mighty power.

Put on the full armor of God so that you can take your stand against the devil's schemes.

For our struggle is not against flesh and blood, but against the rulers, against the authorities, against the powers of this dark world and against the spiritual forces of evil in the heavenly realms.

Therefore put on the full armor of God, so that when the day of evil comes, you may be able to stand your ground, and after you have done everything, to stand.

Stand firm then, with the belt of truth buckled around your waist, with the breastplate of righteousness in place, and with your feet fitted with the readiness that comes from the gospel of peace.

In addition to all this, take up the shield of faith, with which you can extinguish all the flaming arrows of the evil one.

Take the helmet of salvation and the sword of the Spirit, which is the word of God.

And pray in the Spirit on all occasions with all kinds of prayers and requests. With this in mind, be alert and always keep on praying for all the saints.

EPHESIANS 6:10-18, NIV

INSIGHTS FROM MARTIN LUTHER

Where there is to be a true prayer there must be earnestness. Men must feel their distress. Such distress presses them and compels them to call and cry out spontaneously, as prayer ought to be. Then men will require no teaching in how to prepare for it and to attain to the proper devotion.

But the distress that ought to concern us most, both as regards ourselves and everyone, you will find abundantly set forth in the Lord's Prayer. Therefore it is to serve also to remind us of the same, that we contemplate it and lay it to heart, lest we become remiss in prayer. For we all have enough that we lack, but the great want is that we do not feel or see it. Therefore, God also requires that you lament and plead such necessities and wants, not because he does not know them, but that you may kindle your heart to stronger and greater desires, and make wide and open your cloak to receive much.

Therefore, every one of us should accustom himself from his youth daily to pray for all his wants, whenever he is sensible of anything affecting his interests or that of other people among whom he may live, as for preachers, the government, neighbors, domestics, and always (as we have said) to hold up to God his commandment and promise, knowing that he will not have them disregarded.

I would like to see these things brought home again to the

people that they might learn to pray truly and not go about coldly and indifferently, whereby they become daily more unfit for prayer. This is just what the devil desires, and for what he works with all his powers. For he is well aware what damage and harm prayer does to him when it is in proper practice. All our shelter and protection rest in prayer alone. For we are far too feeble to cope with the devil and all his power and adherents that set themselves against us, and they might easily crush us under their feet.

Therefore, we must take up those weapons with which Christians must be armed in order to stand against the devil. For what do you think has hitherto accomplished such great things? What has checked or quelled the counsels, purposes, murder, and riot of our enemies, whereby the devil thought to crush us, together with the gospel, except that the prayer of a few godly men intervened like a wall of iron on our side?

Without prayer they should otherwise have witnessed a far different tragedy, namely, how the devil would have destroyed all Germany in its own blood. But now they may confidently deride it and make a mockery of it. We shall nevertheless be a match for the devil by prayer alone, if we only persevere diligently and not become slack. For whenever a godly Christian prays, "Dear Father, let thy will be done," God speaks from on high and says, "Yes, dear child, it shall be so, in spite of the devil and all the world."

Let this be said as an exhortation, that men may learn, first of all, to esteem prayer as something great and precious, and to make a proper distinction between babbling and praying for something.

—Of Prayer, The Large Catechism

QUESTIONS TO CONSIDER

1. How do you earnestly make your requests known to God?
2. Why does God ask us to pray for what he already knows?

A PRAYERFUL RESPONSE

Lord, teach me to see what I lack from you and ask you for it. Amen.

Hallowed Be Thy Name

THOUGHT FOR TODAY
As God's children, we reflect the holiness of his name.

WISDOM FROM SCRIPTURE
"This, then, is how you should pray: 'Our Father in heaven, hallowed be your name …'"

MATTHEW 6:9, NIV

How great is the love the Father has lavished on us, that we should be called children of God! And that is what we are! The reason the world does not know us is that it did not know him.

Dear friends, now we are children of God, and what we will be has not yet been made known. But we know that when he appears, we shall be like him, for we shall see him as he is.

Everyone who has this hope in him purifies himself, just as he is pure.

Everyone who sins breaks the law; in fact, sin is lawlessness.

But you know that he appeared so that he might take away our sins. And in him is no sin.

No one who lives in him keeps on sinning. No one who continues to sin has either seen him or known him.

Dear children, do not let anyone lead you astray. He who does what is right is righteous, just as he is righteous.

He who does what is sinful is of the devil, because the devil has been sinning from the beginning. The reason the Son of God appeared was to destroy the devil's work.

No one who is born of God will continue to sin, because God's seed remains in him; he cannot go on sinning, because he has been born of God.

This is how we know who the children of God are and who the children of the devil are: Anyone who does not do what is right is not a child of God; nor is anyone who does not love his brother.

This is the message you heard from the beginning: We should love one another.

1 JOHN 3:1-11, NIV

INSIGHTS FROM MARTIN LUTHER

Why do we pray that his name may be holy? Is it not holy already? Yes, it is always holy in its nature, but in our use it is not holy. For God's name was given us when we became Christians and were baptized, so that we are called children of God and have the sacraments by which he so incorporates us in himself that everything which is God's must serve for our use.

Here is the great need for which we ought to be most concerned—that this name have its proper honor, be esteemed holy and sublime as the greatest treasure and sanctuary that we have; and that as godly children we pray that the name of God, which is already holy in heaven, may also be and remain holy with us upon earth and in all the world.

But how does it become holy among us? When both our doctrine and life are godly and Christian. For since in this prayer we call God our Father, it is our duty always to deport ourselves as godly children, that he may not receive shame, but honor and praise from us.

Now the name of God is profaned by us either in words or

in works. (For whatever we do upon the earth must be either words or works, speech or act.) In the first place, then, it is profaned when men preach, teach, and speak in the name of God what is false and misleading, so that his name must serve to adorn and to find a market for falsehood. That is, indeed, the greatest profanation and dishonor of the divine name. It is further dishonored when men—by swearing, cursing, or conjuring—grossly abuse the holy name as a cloak for their shame.

In the second place, the Lord's name is profaned by an openly wicked lifestyle, when those who are called Christians and the people of God are adulterers, drunkards, misers, envious, and slanderers. Here again must the name of God come to shame and be profaned because of us. For just as it is a shame and disgrace to a natural father to have a bad perverse child that opposes him in words and deeds, so that on the child's account he suffers contempt and reproach, so also it brings dishonor upon God if we who are called by his name teach, speak, and live in any other manner except as godly and heavenly children, so that people say of us that we must be not God's but the devil's children.

Thus you see that in this petition we pray just for that which God demands in the Second Commandment; namely, that his name be not taken in vain to swear, curse, lie, and deceive, but be usefully employed to the praise and honor of God. For whoever employs the name of God for any sort of wrong profanes and desecrates this holy name, as in times past when a church was considered desecrated when a murder or any other crime had been committed in it, or when a pyx or relic was desecrated, as being holy in themselves, yet became unholy in use.

This point is easy and clear if only the language is understood, that to hallow is the same as in our idiom to praise, magnify, and honor both in word and deed. How great a need there is of such prayer. Because we see how full the world is of sects and false teachers, who all wear the holy name as a cover and sham for their doctrines of devils, we ought by all means to pray without ceasing, and to cry to and call upon God against all who preach and believe falsely and against whatever opposes and persecutes our gospel and pure doctrine and would suppress it. Likewise, for us who have the Word of God but are not thankful for it, nor live as we ought according to its precepts.

If now you pray for this with your heart, you can be sure that it pleases God, for he will not hear anything more dear to him than that his honor and praise is exalted above everything else, and his Word is taught in its purity and is esteemed precious and dear.

—The Lord's Prayer, The Large Catechism

QUESTIONS TO CONSIDER

1. How do your actions reflect the holiness of God's name?
2. In what ways is God's name defamed through today's culture?

A PRAYERFUL RESPONSE

Lord, show me how to keep your name holy. Amen.

DAY 26

Thy Kingdom Come

THOUGHT FOR TODAY
God desires that we ask for great things from his kingdom.

WISDOM FROM SCRIPTURE
"Your kingdom come ..."

MATTHEW 6:10, NIV

"So I say to you: Ask and it will be given to you; seek and you will find; knock and the door will be opened to you.

"For everyone who asks receives; he who seeks finds; and to him who knocks, the door will be opened.

"Which of you fathers, if your son asks for a fish, will give him a snake instead?

"Or if he asks for an egg, will give him a scorpion?

"If you then, though you are evil, know how to give good gifts to your children, how much more will your Father in heaven give the Holy Spirit to those who ask him!"

LUKE 11:9-13, NIV

INSIGHTS FROM MARTIN LUTHER
Just as the name of God is in itself holy, and we pray nevertheless that it be holy among us, so also his kingdom comes of itself, without our prayer, yet we pray that it may come to us. That is, his name would prevail among us and with us, so that

we may be a part of those among whom his name is hallowed and his kingdom prospers.

But what is the kingdom of God? Nothing else than what we learned in the Creed—that God sent his Son, Jesus Christ our Lord, into the world to redeem and deliver us from the power of the devil and to bring us to himself, and to govern us as a King of righteousness, life, and salvation against sin, death, and an evil conscience, for which end he has also bestowed his Holy Spirit, who is to bring these things home to us by his holy Word, and to illumine and strengthen us in the faith by his power.

Therefore, we pray that this may become effective with us, and that his name be so praised through the holy Word of God and our lives that both we who have accepted his kingdom may abide and daily grow therein, and that it may gain approbation and adherence among other people and proceed with power throughout the world. And that many may find entrance into the Kingdom of Grace and be made partakers of redemption, being led thereto by the Holy Spirit, in order that we may all remain forever in the one kingdom now begun.

For the coming of God's kingdom to us occurs in two ways; first, here in time through the Word and faith; and secondly, in eternity forever through revelation. Now we pray for both of these things, that it may come to those who are not yet in it, and by daily increase, to us who have received the same, and hereafter in eternal life. All this is nothing else than saying: Dear Father, give us first thy Word, that the gospel be preached properly throughout the world.

Secondly, that it be received in faith. That it work and live in us, so that through the Word and the power of the Holy Spirit thy kingdom may prevail among us and the kingdom of the devil be put down, that he may have no right or power over us until at last it shall be utterly destroyed. And sin, death, and hell shall be exterminated, that we may live forever in perfect righteousness and blessedness.

From this you perceive that we pray here not for a crust of bread or a temporal, perishable good, but for an eternal, inestimable treasure and everything that God himself possesses. This is far too great for any human heart to think of desiring if God had not himself commanded us to pray for the same. But because he is God, he also claims the honor of giving more and more abundantly than anyone can comprehend—like an eternal, unfailing fountain, which the more it pours forth and overflows, the more it continues to give. He desires nothing more earnestly of us than that we ask much and great things of him, and again is angry if we do not ask and pray confidently.

For just as when the richest and most mighty emperor would bid a poor beggar ask whatever he might desire, ready to give great imperial presents, and the fool would beg only for a dish of gruel, the beggar would be rightly considered a rogue and a scoundrel who treated the command of his imperial majesty as a jest and sport. He would not be worthy of coming into the emperor's presence. So also it is a great reproach and dishonor to God if we—to whom he offers and pledges so many unspeakable treasures—despise the same or have not the confidence to receive them, but scarcely venture to pray for a piece of bread.

All this is the fault of the shameful unbelief that does not look to God for as much good as will satisfy the stomach, much less expects without doubt such eternal treasures of God. Therefore we must strengthen ourselves against it, and let this be our first prayer. Then, indeed, we shall have all else in abundance, as Christ teaches in Matthew 6:33: "Seek ye first the kingdom of God and his righteousness and all these things shall be added unto you." For how could he allow us to suffer want and to be beggared in temporal things when he promises that which is eternal and imperishable?

—*The Lord's Prayer, The Large Catechism*

QUESTIONS TO CONSIDER

1. Do you ever hesitate to ask God for great things? Why, or why not?
2. How is God's kingdom on earth evident in your life?

A PRAYERFUL RESPONSE

Lord, I want to receive all that you have for me. Amen.

Thy Will Be Done

THOUGHT FOR TODAY

God's agenda will be accomplished.

WISDOM FROM SCRIPTURE

"Your will be done on earth as it is in heaven."

MATTHEW 6:10, NIV

One day the angels came to present themselves before the Lord, and Satan also came with them.

The Lord said to Satan, "Where have you come from?" Satan answered the Lord, "From roaming through the earth and going back and forth in it."

Then the Lord said to Satan, "Have you considered my servant Job? There is no one on earth like him; he is blameless and upright, a man who fears God and shuns evil."

"Does Job fear God for nothing?" Satan replied.

"Have you not put a hedge around him and his household and everything he has? You have blessed the work of his hands, so that his flocks and herds are spread throughout the land.

"But stretch out your hand and strike everything he has, and he will surely curse you to your face."

The Lord said to Satan, "Very well, then, everything he has is in your hands, but on the man himself do not lay a finger." Then Satan went out from the presence of the Lord.

JOB 1:6-12, NIV

Thus far we have prayed that God's name be honored by us, and that his kingdom prevail among us. In these two points is contained all that pertains to the honor of God and to our salvation. But now a need just as great arises, namely, that we do not allow ourselves to be torn from life in God. For as in a good government it is not only necessary that there be those who build and govern well, but also those who make defense, afford protection, and maintain it firmly, the same is true in the spiritual realm.

Although we have prayed for the greatest need—that God may govern us and redeem us from the power of the devil, we must also pray that his will be done. For if we are to abide in his will, we shall have to suffer many thrusts and blows from everything that ventures to oppose and prevent the fulfillment of the two petitions that precede—that God's name be honored and that his kingdom come.

It hurts the devil beyond measure to see his lies and abominations, which have been honored under the most specious pretexts of the divine name, to be exposed so that he is disgraced himself and is driven out of the heart and suffers such a breach in his kingdom. Therefore, he chafes and rages as a fierce enemy with all his power and might, and marshals all his subjects. In addition he enlists the world and our own flesh as his allies. For our flesh is in itself indolent and inclined to evil, even though we have accepted and believed the Word of God. The world, however, is perverse and wicked; this he incites against us and fans and stirs the fire that he may hinder and drive us back, cause us to fall, and again bring us under his power. Such is his will, mind, and every thought, for which he strives day and night and never rests a moment, employing whatever arts, wiles, ways, and means he can invent.

If we would be Christians, therefore, we must surely expect and reckon upon having the devil with all his angels, and the world, as our enemies, who will bring every possible misfortune and grief upon us. For where the Word of God is preached, accepted, or believed, and produces fruit, there the holy cross cannot be wanting. And let no one think that he shall have peace; but he must risk whatever he has upon earth—possessions, honor, house and estate, wife and children, body and life. Now, this hurts our flesh and the old Adam; for the test is to be steadfast and to suffer with patience in whatever way we are assailed, and to let go whatever is taken from us.

Hence there is just as great a need that we pray without ceasing: "Dear Father, thy will be done, not the will of the devil and of our enemies, nor of anything that would persecute and suppress thy holy Word or hinder thy kingdom; and grant that we may bear with patience and overcome whatever is to be endured on that account, lest our poor flesh yield or fall away from weakness or sluggishness."

Whatever we pray concerns only us, namely, that what must be done anyway without us may also be done in us. For as his name must be hallowed and his kingdom come without our prayer, so also his will must be done and succeed, although the devil with all his adherents raise a great tumult and undertake to exterminate the gospel. But for our own sakes we must pray that even against their fury God's will be done without hindrance also among us, that the devil and his army may not be able to accomplish anything, and we remain firm against all violence and persecution, and submit to such the will of God.

—*The Lord's Prayer, The Large Catechism*

QUESTIONS TO CONSIDER
1. How has Satan tried to interfere with God's will in your life?
2. How can prayer arm you for the spiritual battle?

A PRAYERFUL RESPONSE
Lord, help me to stand against anything not of your will in my life. Amen.

Our Daily Bread

THOUGHT FOR TODAY

Our daily bread encompasses more than what we see as a need for today.

WISDOM FROM SCRIPTURE

"Give us today our daily bread."

MATTHEW 6:11, NIV

"Therefore I tell you, do not worry about your life, what you will eat or drink; or about your body, what you will wear. Is not life more important than food, and the body more important than clothes?

"Look at the birds of the air; they do not sow or reap or store away in barns, and yet your heavenly Father feeds them. Are you not much more valuable than they?

"Who of you by worrying can add a single hour to his life?

"And why do you worry about clothes? See how the lilies of the field grow. They do not labor or spin.

"Yet I tell you that not even Solomon in all his splendor was dressed like one of these.

"If that is how God clothes the grass of the field, which is here today and tomorrow is thrown into the fire, will he not much more clothe you, O you of little faith?

"So do not worry, saying, 'What shall we eat?' or 'What shall we drink?' or 'What shall we wear?'

"For the pagans run after all these things, and your heavenly Father knows that you need them.

"But seek first his kingdom and his righteousness, and all these things will be given to you as well.

"Therefore do not worry about tomorrow, for tomorrow will worry about itself. Each day has enough trouble of its own."

MATTHEW 6:25-34, NIV

INSIGHTS FROM MARTIN LUTHER

Here, now, we consider the poor breadbasket, the necessaries of our body and of the temporal life. It is a brief and simple word, but it has a very wide scope. For when you mention and pray for daily bread, you pray for everything that is necessary in order to have and enjoy daily bread and, on the other hand, against everything that interferes with it.

Therefore, you must open wide and extend your thoughts not only to the oven or the flour bin but to the distant field and the entire land, which bears and brings to us daily bread and every sort of sustenance. For if God did not cause it to grow, and bless and preserve it in the field, we could never take bread from the oven or have any to set upon the table.

To comprise it briefly, this petition includes everything that belongs to our entire life in the world, because on that account alone do we need daily bread. Now for our life it is not only necessary that our body have food and covering and other necessities, but also that we spend our days in peace and quiet among the people with whom we live and communicate in daily business and conversation and all sorts of doings. In short, whatever pertains both to the domestic and to the neighborly or civil relation and government. For where these two things are hindered [intercepted and disturbed] that they do not prosper as they ought, the necessities of life also are impeded, so that ultimately life cannot be maintained. And there is, indeed, the greatest need to pray for temporal authority and government, as that by which most of all God preserves to us our daily bread and all the comforts of this life. For though we have received of God all good things in abundance, we are not able to retain any of them or use them in security and happiness if he did not give us a permanent and peaceful government. For where there are dissension, strife, and war, there the daily bread is already taken away, or at least checked.

Therefore, it would be very proper to place in the coat of arms of every pious prince a loaf of bread instead of a lion, or a wreath of rue, or to stamp it upon the coin, to remind both them and their subjects that by their office we have protection and peace, and that without them we could not eat and retain our daily bread. Therefore, they are also worthy of all honor that we give to them for their office, as to those through whom we enjoy in peace and quietness what we have, because otherwise we would not keep a farthing. In addition, we also pray for them that through them God may bestow on us the more blessing and good.

Let this be a very brief explanation and sketch, showing how far this petition extends through all conditions on earth. Of this anyone might indeed make a long prayer, and with many words enumerate all the things that are included therein, as we pray God to give us food and drink, clothing, house and home, and health of body; also that he cause the grain and fruits of the field to grow and mature well; furthermore, that he help us at home towards good housekeeping, that he give and preserve to us a godly wife, children, and servants; that he cause our work, trade, or whatever we are engaged in to prosper and succeed, and favor us with faithful neighbors and good friends. Likewise, that he give to emperors, kings, and all estates, and especially to the rulers of our country and to all counselors, magistrates, and officers, wisdom, strength, and success that they may govern well and vanquish the Turks and all enemies; to subjects and the common people obedience, peace, and harmony in their life with one another, and on the other hand, that he would preserve us from all sorts of calamity to body and livelihood, as lightning, hail, fire, flood, poison, pestilence, cattle-plague, war and bloodshed, famine, destructive beasts, wicked men. All this it is well to impress upon the simple, namely, that these things come from God and must be prayed for by us.

This petition is especially directed also against our chief enemy, the devil. For all his thought and desire is to deprive us of all that we have from God, or to hinder it; and he is not satisfied to obstruct and destroy spiritual government in leading souls astray by his lies and bringing them under his power. He also prevents and hinders the stability of all government and honorable, peaceable relations on earth. There he causes so much contention, murder, sedition, and war; also, lightning and hail to destroy grain and cattle, to poison the air, etc. In short, he is sorry that anyone has a morsel of bread from God and eats it in peace; and if it were in his power, and our prayer (next to God) did not prevent him, we would not keep a straw in the field, a farthing in the house, yea, not even our life for an hour, especially those who have the Word of God and would like to be Christians.

Thus God wishes to indicate to us how he cares for us in all our need and faithfully provides also for our temporal support. Although he abundantly grants and preserves these things even to the wicked and knaves, yet he wishes that we pray for them, in order that we may recognize that we receive them from his hand and may feel his paternal goodness toward us therein. For when he withdraws his hand, nothing can prosper nor be maintained in the end, as, indeed, we daily see and experience. How much trouble there is now in the world on account of bad coin, yea, on account of daily oppression and raising of prices in common trade, bargaining and labor on the part of those who wantonly oppress the poor and deprive them of their daily bread! This we must suffer indeed; but let them take care that they do not lose the common intercession, and beware lest this petition in the Lord's Prayer be against them.

—*The Lord's Prayer, The Large Catechism*

QUESTIONS TO CONSIDER
1. How can you better pray for those in government authority?
2. How has God provided for your needs?

A PRAYERFUL RESPONSE
Lord, thank you for faithfully providing for my needs. Amen.

Forgive Us, Father

THOUGHT FOR TODAY

We must forgive to be forgiven.

WISDOM FROM SCRIPTURE

"Forgive us our debts, as we also have forgiven our debtors."

MATTHEW 6:12, NIV

"Therefore, the kingdom of heaven is like a king who wanted to settle accounts with his servants.

"As he began the settlement, a man who owed him ten thousand talents was brought to him.

"Since he was not able to pay, the master ordered that he and his wife and his children and all that he had be sold to repay the debt.

"The servant fell on his knees before him. 'Be patient with me,' he begged, 'and I will pay back everything.'

"The servant's master took pity on him, canceled the debt and let him go.

"But when that servant went out, he found one of his fellow servants who owed him a hundred denarii. He grabbed him and began to choke him. 'Pay back what you owe me!' he demanded.

"His fellow servant fell to his knees and begged him, 'Be patient with me, and I will pay you back.'

"But he refused. Instead, he went off and had the man thrown into prison until he could pay the debt.

"When the other servants saw what had happened, they were greatly distressed and went and told their master everything that had happened.

"Then the master called the servant in. 'You wicked servant,' he said, 'I canceled all that debt of yours because you begged me to.

"'Shouldn't you have had mercy on your fellow servant just as I had on you?'

"In anger his master turned him over to the jailers to be tortured, until he should pay back all he owed.

"This is how my heavenly Father will treat each of you unless you forgive your brother from your heart."

MATTHEW 18:23-35, NIV

INSIGHTS FROM MARTIN LUTHER

This part now relates to our poor miserable life, which, although we have and believe the Word of God, and do and submit to his will, and are supported by his gifts and blessings, is nevertheless not without sin. For we still stumble daily and transgress because we live in the world among men who do us much harm and give us cause for impatience, anger, revenge, etc. Besides, we have Satan at our back, who sets upon us on every side and fights against all the foregoing petitions, so that it is not possible always to stand firm in such a persistent conflict.

Therefore, there is here again great need to call upon God and to pray: Dear Father, forgive us our trespasses. Not as though he did not forgive sin without, and even before, our prayer (for he has given us the gospel, in which is pure forgiveness before we prayed or ever thought about it). But this is to the intent that we may recognize and accept such forgiveness. For the flesh in which we daily live is of such a nature that it neither trusts nor believes God, and is ever active in evil lusts and devices so that we sin daily in word and deed, by commission and omission, by which the conscience is thrown into unrest so that it is afraid of the wrath and displeasure of God, and thus loses the comfort and confidence derived from the gospel. Therefore, it is ceaselessly necessary that we run hither and obtain consolation to comfort the conscience again.

But this should serve God's purpose of breaking our pride and keeping us humble. For in case anyone should boast of his godliness and despise others, God has reserved this prerogative to himself, that the person is to consider himself and place this prayer before his eyes. He will find that he is no better than others, and that in the presence of God all must lower their plumes and be glad that they can attain forgiveness. And let no one think that as long as we live here he can reach such a position that he will not need such forgiveness. In short, if God does not forgive without ceasing, we are lost.

It is therefore the intent of this petition that God would not regard our sins and hold up to us what we daily deserve, but would deal graciously with us and forgive, as he has promised, and thus grant us a joyful and confident conscience to stand before him in prayer. For where the heart is not in right relation toward God, nor can take such confidence, it will nevermore venture to pray. But such a confident and joyful heart can spring from nothing else than the [certain] knowledge of the forgiveness of sin.

But there is here attached a necessary yet consolatory addition: As we forgive, he has promised that we shall be sure that everything is forgiven and pardoned, yet in the manner that we also forgive our neighbor. For just as we daily sin much against God, and yet he forgives everything through grace, so we, too, must ever forgive our neighbor who does us injury, violence, and wrong. If, therefore, you do not forgive, then do not think that God forgives you. But if you forgive, you have this consolation and assurance that you are forgiven in heaven, not on account of your forgiving—for God forgives freely and without condition out of pure grace because he has so promised—but in order that he may set this up for our confirmation and assurance for a sign alongside of the promise which accords with this prayer in Luke 6:37: Forgive, and ye shall be forgiven. Therefore, Christ also repeats it soon after the Lord's Prayer and says in Matthew 6:14: For if ye forgive men their trespasses, your heavenly Father will also forgive you.

This sign is therefore attached to this petition, that, when we pray, we remember the promise and reflect thus: Dear Father, for this reason I come and pray you to forgive me, not that I can merit anything by my works, but because you have promised and attached the seal to my asking that I should be as sure as though I had absolution pronounced by you. For as much as baptism and the Lord's Supper are appointed as external signs, so much also this sign can effect to confirm our consciences and cause them to rejoice. And it is especially given for this purpose, that we might use and practice it every hour as a thing that we have with us at all times.

—*The Lord's Prayer, The Large Catechism*

QUESTIONS TO CONSIDER

1. Is there someone from whom you need to ask forgiveness?
2. What steps need to be taken for reconciliation?

A PRAYERFUL RESPONSE

Lord, bring to mind any person or situation where I need to forgive. Amen.

Deliver Us From Evil

THOUGHT FOR TODAY

God gives us the power to resist temptation and be delivered from evil.

WISDOM FROM SCRIPTURE

"And lead us not into temptation, but deliver us from the evil one."

MATTHEW 6:13, NIV

Your statutes are wonderful; therefore I obey them.

The unfolding of your words gives light; it gives understanding to the simple.

I open my mouth and pant, longing for your commands.

Turn to me and have mercy on me, as you always do to those who love your name.

Direct my footsteps according to your word; let no sin rule over me.

Redeem me from the oppression of men, that I may obey your precepts.

Make your face shine upon your servant and teach me your decrees.

Streams of tears flow from my eyes, for your law is not obeyed.

Righteous are you, O Lord, and your laws are right.

The statutes you have laid down are righteous; they are fully trustworthy.

PSALM 119:129-38, NIV

No temptation has seized you except what is common to man. And God is faithful; he will not let you be tempted beyond what you can bear. But when you are tempted, he will also provide a way out so that you can stand up under it.

1 CORINTHIANS 10:13, NIV

INSIGHTS FROM MARTIN LUTHER

We have now heard enough about what toil and labor is required to retain all that for which we pray, and to persevere therein, which is not achieved without infirmities and stumbling. Although we have received forgiveness and a good conscience, and are entirely acquitted, yet is the nature of life that one stands today and tomorrow falls. Therefore, even though we be godly now and stand before God with a good conscience, we must pray again that he would not allow us to relapse and yield to trials and temptations.

Temptation, however, is of three kinds, namely, of the flesh, of the world, and of the devil. For in the flesh we dwell and carry the old Adam about our neck, who exerts himself and incites us daily to moral impurity, laziness, gluttony and drunkenness, avarice and deception, to defraud our neighbor and to overcharge him, and, in short, to all manner of evil lusts that cleave to us by nature, and to which we are incited by the society, example, and what we hear and see of other people, which often wound and inflame even an innocent heart.

Next comes the world, which offends us in word and deed, and impels us to anger and impatience. In short, there is nothing but hatred and envy, enmity, violence and wrong, unfaithfulness, vengeance, cursing, raillery, slander, pride and haughtiness, with superfluous finery, honor, fame, and power, where no one is willing to be the least, but everyone desires to sit at the head and to be seen before all.

Then comes the devil, inciting and provoking in all directions, but especially agitating matters that concern the conscience and spiritual affairs, namely, to induce us to despise and disregard both the Word and works of God to tear us away from faith, hope, and love and bring us into misbelief, false security, and obduracy. Or, on the other hand, to despair, denial of God, blasphemy, and innumerable other shocking things. These are indeed snares and nets, yea, real fiery darts which are shot most venomously into the heart, not by flesh and blood, but by the devil.

Great and grievous, indeed, are these dangers and temptations which every Christian must bear, even though each one were alone by himself, so that every hour that we are in this vile life we are attacked on all sides, chased and hunted down. We are moved to cry out and to pray that God would not allow us to become weary and faint and to relapse into sin, shame, and unbelief. For otherwise it is impossible to overcome even the least temptation.

This, then, is leading us not into temptation, to wit, when he gives us power and strength to resist the temptation without it being taken away or removed. For while we live in the flesh and have the devil about us, no one can escape temptation and allurements; and it cannot be otherwise than that we must endure trials, yea, be engulfed in them; but we pray for this, that we may not fall and be drowned in them.

To feel temptation is a far different thing from consenting or yielding to it. We must all feel it, although not all in the same manner, but some in a greater degree and more severely than others; as the young suffer especially from the flesh. Afterwards, they that attain to middle life and old age, suffer from the world. Others, who are occupied with spiritual matters, that is, strong Christians, suffer from the devil. But such feeling, as long as it is against our will and we would rather be rid of it, can harm no one. For if we did not feel it, it could not be called a temptation. But to consent to it is when we give it the reins and do not resist or pray against it.

Therefore, we finally sum it all up and say: Dear Father, help us that we be rid of all these calamities. But there is also included whatever evil may happen to us under the devil's kingdom—poverty, shame, death, and, in short, all the agonizing misery and heartache of which there is such an unnumbered multitude on the earth. For since the devil is not only a liar, but also a murderer, he constantly seeks our lives and wreaks his anger whenever he can afflict our bodies with misfortune and harm. Hence it comes that he often breaks men's necks or drives them to insanity, drowns some, and incites many to commit suicide and to many other terrible calamities. There is nothing for us to do upon earth but to pray against this archenemy without ceasing. For unless God preserved us, we would not be safe from him even for an hour.

Hence you see again how God wishes us to pray to him for all the things which affect our bodily interests, so that we seek and expect help nowhere else except in him. But this matter he has put last; for if we are to be preserved and delivered from all evil, the name of God must first be hallowed in us, his kingdom must be with us, and his will be done. After that he will finally preserve us from sin and shame, and, besides, from everything that may hurt or injure us.

—*The Lord's Prayer, The Large Catechism*

QUESTIONS TO CONSIDER

1. In what areas of life are you most tempted?
2. How do you draw on God's strength for deliverance?

A PRAYERFUL RESPONSE

Lord, lead me out of temptation into deliverance. Amen.

PART FOUR

Obeying the Commands

May God bestow on us his grace,
With blessings rich provide us,
And may the brightness of his face
To life eternal guide us
That we his saving health may know,
His gracious will and pleasure,
And also to the heathen show
Christ's riches without measure
And unto God convert them.

Oh, let the people praise thy worth,
In all good works increasing;
The land shall plenteous fruit bring forth,
Thy Word is rich in blessing.
May God the Father, God the Son,
And God the Spirit bless us!
Let all the world praise him alone,
Let solemn awe possess us.
Now let our hearts say, Amen.

From "May God Bestow on Us His Grace"
by Martin Luther

MARTIN LUTHER'S INSIGHT

The Lord's commands form the path to righteousness.

DAY 31

With Your Whole Heart

THOUGHT FOR TODAY

Our confidence and trust is in God alone.

WISDOM FROM SCRIPTURE

I am the Lord your God, who brought you out of the land of Egypt, out of the house of slavery; you shall have no other gods before me.

EXODUS 20:2-3, NRSV

One of the scribes came near and heard them disputing with one another, and seeing that he answered them well, he asked him, "Which commandment is the first of all?"

Jesus answered, "The first is, 'Hear, O Israel: the Lord our God, the Lord is one; you shall love the Lord your God with all your heart, and with all your soul, and with all your mind, and with all your strength.'

"The second is this, 'You shall love your neighbor as yourself.' There is no other commandment greater than these."

Then the scribe said to him, "You are right, Teacher; you have truly said that 'he is one, and besides him there is no other'; and 'to love him with all the heart, and with all the understanding, and with all the strength,' and 'to love one's neighbor as oneself'—this is much more important than all whole burnt offerings and sacrifices."

When Jesus saw that he answered wisely, he said to him,

"You are not far from the kingdom of God." After that no one dared to ask him any question.

MARK 12:28-34, NRSV

INSIGHTS FROM MARTIN LUTHER

Thou shalt have [and worship] me alone as your God. What is the force of this, and how is it to be understood? What does it mean to have a god? or, what is God? Answer: A god means that from which we are to expect all good and to which we are to take refuge in all distress, so that to have a God is nothing else than to trust and believe him from the [whole] heart. As I have often said, the confidence and faith of the heart alone make both God and an idol. If your faith and trust be right, then is your god also true; and, on the other hand, if your trust be false and wrong, then you have not the true God, for these two belong together—faith and God. That upon which you set your heart and put your trust is properly your god.

Therefore, it is the intent of this commandment to require true faith and trust of the heart which settles upon the only true God and clings to him alone. That is as much as to say: "See to it that you let me alone be your God, and never seek another," i.e.: Whatever you lack of good things, expect it of me, and look to me for it, and whenever you suffer misfortune and distress, creep and cling to me. I, yes, I, will give you enough and help you out of every need; only let not your heart cleave to or rest in any other.

Many a person thinks that he has God and everything in **abundance** when he has money and possessions; he trusts in them and boasts of them with such firmness and assurance as to care for no one. Lo, such a man also has a god, Mammon by name, which is money and possessions. On these he sets his

153

heart. The love of money is the most common idol on earth.

He who has money and possessions feels secure, and is joyful and undismayed as though he were sitting in the midst of Paradise. On the other hand, he who has no money or possessions doubts and is despondent, as though he knew of no God. For very few are to be found who are of good cheer and who neither mourn nor complain if they have not Mammon. This [care and desire for money] sticks and clings to our nature, even to the grave.

So, too, whoever trusts and boasts that he possesses great skill, prudence, power, favor, friendship and honor has also a god, but not this true and only God. This appears again when you notice how presumptuous, secure, and proud people are because of such possessions, and how despondent when they no longer exist or are withdrawn. Therefore, I repeat that the chief explanation of this point is that to have a god is to have something in which the heart entirely trusts.

Here you have the meaning of the true honor and worship of God, which pleases God and which he commands under penalty of eternal wrath, namely, that the heart knows no other comfort or confidence than in him and does not allow itself to be torn from him but, for him, risks and disregards everything upon earth. On the other hand, you can easily see and judge how the world practices only false worship and idolatry. For no people has ever been so reprobate as not to institute and observe some divine worship; everyone has set up as his special god whatever he looked to for blessings, help, and comfort.

But let this be said to the simple, that they may well note and remember the meaning of this commandment, namely, that we are to trust in God alone and look to him and expect from him nothing but good, as from one who gives us body, life, food, drink, nourishment, health, protection, peace, and all necessities of both temporal and eternal things. He also preserves us from misfortune, and if any evil befall us, delivers and rescues us, so that it is God alone from whom we receive all good, and by whom we are delivered from evil.

Let us, then, learn well the First Commandment, that we may see how God will tolerate no presumption nor any trust in any other object, and how he requires nothing higher of us than confidence from the heart for everything good, so that we may use all the blessings which God gives no farther than as a shoemaker uses his needle, awl, and thread for work, and then lays them aside. Or as a traveler uses an inn, and food, and his bed only for temporal necessity. Each one in his station, according to God's order, and without allowing any of these things to be our food or idol. Let this suffice with respect to the First Commandment, which we have had to explain at length, since it is of chief importance because where the heart is rightly disposed toward God and this commandment is observed, all the others follow.

—*The First Commandment, The Large Catechism*

QUESTIONS TO CONSIDER

1. Do you trust anyone or anything more than God?
2. Today, how can you honor God more?

A PRAYERFUL RESPONSE

Lord, I want to trust you fully. Amen.

DAY 32

The Name Above All Names

THOUGHT FOR TODAY

God's name is given for proper use by his children.

WISDOM FROM SCRIPTURE

You shall not make wrongful use of the name of the Lord your God, for the Lord will not acquit anyone who misuses his name.

EXODUS 20:7, NRSV

"Again, you have heard that it was said to those of ancient times, 'You shall not swear falsely, but carry out the vows you have made to the Lord.'

But I say to you, Do not swear at all, either by heaven, for it is the throne of God,

Or by the earth, for it is his footstool, or by Jerusalem, for it is the city of the great King.

And do not swear by your head, for you cannot make one hair white or black.

Let your word be 'Yes, Yes' or 'No, No'; anything more than this comes from the evil one.

MATTHEW 5:33-37, NRSV

You that boast in the law, do you dishonor God by breaking the law?

For, as it is written, "The name of God is blasphemed among the Gentiles because of you."

ROMANS 2:23-24, NRSV

Thou shalt not take the name of the Lord, thy God, in vain.

As the First Commandment has instructed the heart and taught [the basis of] faith, so this commandment leads us forth and directs the mouth and tongue to God. For the first objects that spring from the heart and manifest themselves are words. Now, as I have taught how to answer the question, what it is to have a god, so you must learn to comprehend simply the meaning of this and all the commandments, and to apply it to yourself.

If, then, it be asked: How do you understand the Second Commandment, or what is meant by taking in vain, or misusing, God's name? Answer briefly thus: It is misusing God's name when we call upon the Lord God, no matter in what way, for purposes of falsehood or wrong of any kind. Therefore, this commandment enjoins this much, that God's name must not be appealed to falsely or taken upon the lips while the heart knows well enough, or should know, differently; as among those who take oaths in court, where one side lies against the other. For God's name cannot be misused worse than for the support of falsehood and deceit.

From this everyone can readily infer when and in how many ways God's name is misused, although it is impossible to enumerate all its misuses. Yet, to tell it in a few words, all misuse of the divine name occurs, first, in worldly business and in matters which concern money, possessions, honor, whether it be publicly in court, in the market, or wherever else men make false oaths in God's name or pledge their souls in any matter. And this is especially prevalent in marriage affairs where two go and secretly betroth themselves to one another, and afterward abjure [their plighted troth]. But the greatest abuse occurs in spiritual matters, which pertain to the conscience, when false preachers rise up and offer their lying vanities as God's Word.

Behold, all this is decking one's self out with God's name, or making a pretty show, or claiming to be right, whether it occur in gross, worldly business or in sublime, subtile matters of faith and doctrine. And among liars belong also blasphemers, not alone those who disgrace God's name without fear (these are not for us, but for the hangman to discipline); but also those who publicly malign the truth and God's Word and consign it to the devil. Of this there is no need now to speak further.

Here, then, let us learn and take to heart the great importance of this commandment, that with all diligence we may guard against and dread every misuse of the holy name as the greatest sin that can be outwardly committed. For to lie and deceive is in itself a great sin, but is greatly aggravated when we attempt to justify it and seek to confirm it by invoking the name of God and using it as a cloak for shame, so that from a single lie a double lie, nay, manifold lies, result.

For this reason, too, God has added a solemn threat to this commandment, to wit: For the Lord will not hold him guiltless who takes his name in vain. That is, it shall not be condoned to anyone nor pass unpunished. For as little as he will leave it unavenged if anyone turn his heart from him, as little will he suffer his name to be employed for dressing up a lie. Now alas! it is a common calamity in all the world that there are as few who are not using the name of God for purposes of lying and all wickedness as there are those who with their hearts trust alone in God.

Therefore, I advise and exhort as before that by means of warning and threatening, restraint and punishment, the children be trained to shun falsehood, and especially to avoid the use of God's name in its support. For where they are allowed to do as they please, no good will result. It is even now evident that the world is worse than it has ever been and that there is no government, no obedience, no fidelity, no faith, but only daring, unbridled men, whom no teaching or reproof helps—all of which is God's wrath and punishment for such wanton contempt of this commandment.

On the other hand, they should be constantly urged and incited to honor God's name, and to have it always upon their lips in everything that may happen to them or come to their notice: For that is the true honor of his name, to look to it and implore it for all consolation, so that first the heart by faith gives God the honor due him, and afterwards the lips by confession.

—*The Second Commandment, The Large Catechism*

QUESTIONS TO CONSIDER

1. What does it mean to use God's name in vain?
2. How can you recognize when you invoke God's name improperly?

A PRAYERFUL RESPONSE

Lord, may I honor your name with my lips and my life. Amen.

DAY 33

Remembering the Holy

THOUGHT FOR TODAY

God provides us with a holy day of rest.

WISDOM FROM SCRIPTURE

Remember the sabbath day, and keep it holy.

Six days you shall labor and do all your work.

But the seventh day is a sabbath to the Lord your God; you shall not do any work—you, your son or your daughter, your male or female slave, your livestock, or the alien resident in your towns.

EXODUS 20:8-10, NRSV

One sabbath he was going through the grainfields; and as they made their way his disciples began to pluck heads of grain.

The Pharisees said to him, "Look, why are they doing what is not lawful on the sabbath?"

And he said to them, "Have you never read what David did when he and his companions were hungry and in need of food?

He entered the house of God, when Abiathar was high priest, and ate the bread of the Presence, which it is not lawful for any but the priests to eat, and he gave some to his companions."

Then he said to them, "The sabbath was made for humankind, and not humankind for the sabbath; so the Son of Man is lord even of the sabbath."

MARK 2:23-28, NRSV

Thou shalt sanctify the holy day. [Remember the Sabbath day to keep it holy.]

The word *holy day* is rendered from the Hebrew word *sabbath*, which properly signifies to rest, that is, to abstain from labor. Hence we are accustomed to say, *Feierbend machen* [that is, to cease working], or *heiligen Abend geben* [sanctify the Sabbath]. Now, in the Old Testament, God separated the seventh day and appointed it for rest and commanded that it should be regarded as holy above all others. As regards this external observance, this commandment was given to the Jews alone, that they should abstain from toilsome work, and rest, so that both man and beast might recuperate and not be weakened by unremitting labor. Although they afterwards restricted this too closely, and grossly abused it, so that they misrepresented it and could not endure in Christ those works which they themselves were accustomed to do on that day, as we read in the gospel, just as though the commandment were fulfilled by doing no external [manual] work whatever, which was not the meaning—that they sanctify the holy day or day of rest.

This commandment, therefore, according to its gross sense, does not concern us Christians; for it is altogether an external matter, like other ordinances of the Old Testament, which were attached to particular customs, persons, times, and places, and now have been made free through Christ.

But to grasp a Christian meaning for the simple as to what God requires in this commandment, note that we keep holy days not for the sake of intelligent and learned Christians (for they have no need of it [holy days]), but first of all for bodily causes and necessities, which nature teaches and requires. It is for the common people, menservants and maidservants, who have been attending to their work and trade the whole week, that for a day they may retire in order to rest and be refreshed.

Secondly, and most especially, that on such day of rest (since we can get no other opportunity), freedom and time be taken to attend church, so that we come together to hear and learn of God and then to praise God, to sing and pray.

However, this, I say, is not so restricted to any time, as with the Jews, that it must be just on this or that day, for in itself no one day is better than another; but this should indeed be done daily. However, since the masses cannot give such attendance, there must be at least one day in the week set apart. By tradition, Sunday [the Lord's Day] has been appointed for this purpose, and we also should continue the same in order that everything be done in harmonious order and no one create disorder by unnecessary innovation.

Therefore, this is the simple meaning of the commandment: Since holy days are observed anyhow, such observance should be devoted to hearing God's Word, so that the special function of this day should be the ministry of the Word for the young and the mass of poor people, yet that the resting be not so strictly interpreted as to forbid any other incidental work that cannot be avoided.

Accordingly, when asked, What is meant by the commandment: Thou shalt sanctify the holy day? Answer that it is the same as to keep it holy. But what is meant by keeping it holy? Nothing else than to be occupied in holy words, works, and life. For the day needs no sanctification for itself, for in itself it has been created holy [from the beginning of the creation it was sanctified by its Creator]. But God desires it to be holy to you. Therefore, it becomes holy or unholy on your account, according as you are occupied on the same with things that are holy or unholy.

How, then, does such sanctification take place? Not in this manner, that [with folded hands] we sit behind the stove and do no rough [external] work, or deck ourselves with a wreath and put on our best clothes, but that we occupy ourselves with God's Word, and exercise ourselves therein.

Indeed, we Christians ought always to keep such a holy day and be occupied with nothing but holy things, i.e., daily be engaged upon God's Word and carry it in our hearts and upon our lips. But since we do not at all times have leisure, we must devote several hours a week for the sake of the young, or at least a day for the sake of the entire multitude, to being concerned about this alone, and especially urge the Ten Commandments, the Creed, and the Lord's Prayer, and thus direct our whole life and being according to God's Word.

At whatever time, then, this is being observed and practiced, there a true holy day is being kept; otherwise it shall not be called a Christians' holy day.

For the Word of God is the sanctuary above all sanctuaries, yea, the only one which we Christians know and have. For though we had the bones of all the saints or all holy and consecrated garments upon a heap, it would not sanctify us, for all that is a dead thing which can sanctify nobody. But God's Word is the treasure which sanctifies everything, and by which even all the saints themselves were sanctified. At whatever hour then, God's Word is taught, preached, heard, read, or meditated upon, there the person, day, and work are sanctified, not because of the external work but because of the Word which makes saints of us all. Therefore, I constantly say that all our life and work must be ordered according to God's Word if it is to be God-pleasing or holy. Where this is done, this commandment is in force and being fulfilled.

—*The Third Commandment, The Large Catechism*

QUESTIONS TO CONSIDER

1. How do you observe the sabbath?
2. Is your sabbath restful? Why or why not?

A PRAYERFUL RESPONSE

Lord, I offer my sabbath as a day of rest to you. Amen.

A Matter of Honor

THOUGHT FOR TODAY
Honoring our parents comes with a promise.

WISDOM FROM SCRIPTURE
Honor your father and your mother, so that your days may be long in the land that the Lord your God is giving you.

EXODUS 20:12, NRSV

Then Pharisees and scribes came to Jesus from Jerusalem and said,

"Why do your disciples break the tradition of the elders? For they do not wash their hands before they eat."

He answered them, "And why do you break the commandment of God for the sake of your tradition?

"For God said, 'Honor your father and your mother,' and, 'Whoever speaks evil of father or mother must surely die.'

"But you say that whoever tells father or mother, 'Whatever support you might have had from me is given to God, then that person need not honor the father.

"So, for the sake of your tradition, you make void the word of God.

"You hypocrites! Isaiah prophesied rightly about you when he said:
'This people honors me with their lips,
but their hearts are far from me;
in vain do they worship me,

teaching human precepts as doctrines.'"

Then he called the crowd to him and said to them, "Listen and understand: it is not what goes into the mouth that defiles a person, but it is what comes out of the mouth that defiles."

MATTHEW 15:1-11, NRSV

INSIGHTS FROM MARTIN LUTHER

Thou shalt honor thy father and thy mother.

To this estate of fatherhood and motherhood God has given the special distinction above all estates that are beneath it. He commands us not only to love our parents, but to honor them. For with respect to brothers, sisters, and our neighbors in general, he commands nothing higher than that we love them, so that he separates and distinguishes father and mother above all other persons upon earth and places them at his side.

It is a far higher thing to honor than to love. Honor comprehends not only love but also modesty, humility, and deference, and requires not only that parents be addressed kindly and with reverence, but most of all that both in heart and with the body we so act as to show that we esteem them very highly, and that next to God we regard them as the very highest. For one whom we are to honor from the heart we must truly regard as high and great.

We must impress it upon the young that they should regard their parents as in God's stead and remember that however lowly, poor, frail, and odd they may be, nevertheless they are father and mother given them by God. Our parents are not to be deprived of their honor because of their conduct or their failings. Therefore, we are not to regard their persons, how they may be, but the will of God who has thus created and ordained.

In other respects we are, indeed, all alike in the eyes of God; but among us there must necessarily be such inequality and ordered difference, and therefore God commands it to be observed that you obey me as your father, and that I have the supremacy.

Learn, first, what is the honor toward parents required by this commandment—that they be held in distinction and esteem above all things as the most precious treasure on earth. Furthermore, that in our words we observe modesty toward them, do not accost them roughly, haughtily, and defiantly, but yield to them and be silent even though they go too far. Thirdly, that we show them such honor with our body and possessions that we serve them, help them, and provide for them when they are old, sick, infirm, or poor, and that we do it gladly, with humility and reverence, as doing it before God. For he who knows how to regard them in his heart will not allow them to suffer want or hunger, but will place them above him and at his side, and will share with them whatever he has and possesses.

Notice how great, good, and holy a work is here assigned children, which is alas! utterly neglected and disregarded, and no one perceives that God has commanded it or that it is a holy, divine word and doctrine. For if it had been regarded as such, everyone could have inferred that they must be holy men who live according to these words. There would have been no need of inventing monasticism nor spiritual orders, but every child would have abided by this commandment and could have directed his conscience to God and said: "If I am to do good and holy works, I know of none better than to render all honor and obedience to my parents, because God has himself commanded it. For what God commands must be far nobler than everything that we may devise ourselves. Since there is no higher or better teacher to be found than God, there can be no better doctrine than he gives forth."

Behold, in this manner we would have had a godly child properly taught, reared in true blessedness, and kept at home in obedience to his parents and in their service, so that men should have had blessing and joy from the spectacle. However, God's commandment was not permitted to be thus [with such care and diligence] commended, but had to be neglected and trampled under foot, so that a child could not lay it to heart, and meanwhile gaped [like a panting wolf] at the devices which we set up, without once [consulting or] giving reverence to God.

Let us, therefore, learn at last, for God's sake, that placing all other things out of sight, our youths look first to this commandment if they wish to serve God with truly good works and do what is pleasing to their fathers and mothers, or to those to whom they may be subject in their stead. For every child who knows and does this has this great consolation in his heart that he can joyfully say and boast, "Behold, this work is well pleasing to my God in heaven, that I know for certain."

Therefore, you should be heartily glad and thank God that he has chosen you and made you worthy to do a work so precious and pleasing to him. Only see that, although it be regarded as the most humble and despised, you esteem it great and precious, not on account of our worthiness, but because it is comprehended in and controlled by the Word and commandment of God.

Those who keep in sight God's will and commandment have the promise that everything which they bestow upon temporal and spiritual fathers, and whatever they do to honor them, shall be richly recompensed to them. They shall have, not bread, clothing, and money for a year or two, but long life, support, and peace, and shall be eternally rich and blessed. Therefore, only do what is your duty, and let God take care how he is to support you and provide for you sufficiently. Since he has promised it, and has never yet lied, he will not be found lying to you.

—The Fourth Commandment, The Large Catechism

QUESTIONS TO CONSIDER

1. Why is it sometimes difficult to honor our parents?
2. Why is honoring them so important to God?

A PRAYERFUL RESPONSE

Lord, I want to honor my parents, even if they are no longer part of my daily life. Amen.

To Do No Harm

THOUGHT FOR TODAY

Murder begins in the heart.

WISDOM FROM SCRIPTURE

You shall not murder.

EXODUS 20:13, NRSV

"Therefore, whoever breaks one of the least of these commandments, and teaches others to do the same, will be called least in the kingdom of heaven; but whoever does them and teaches them will be called great in the kingdom of heaven.

"For I tell you, unless your righteousness exceeds that of the scribes and Pharisees, you will never enter the kingdom of heaven.

"You have heard that it was said to those of ancient times, 'You shall not murder'; and 'whoever murders shall be liable to judgment.'

"But I say to you that if you are angry with a brother or sister, you will be liable to judgment; and if you insult a brother or sister, you will be liable to the council; and if you say, 'You fool,' you will be liable to the hell of fire.

"So when you are offering your gift at the altar, if you remember that your brother or sister has something against you, leave your gift there before the altar and go; first be reconciled to your brother or sister, and then come and offer your gift."

MATTHEW 5:19-24, NRSV

Thou shalt not kill.

Now, this commandment is easy enough and has been often treated, because we hear it annually in the Gospel of Matthew 5:21ff., where Christ himself explains and sums it up, namely, that we must not kill neither with hand, heart, mouth, signs, gestures, help, nor counsel. Therefore, it is here forbidden to everyone to be angry, except those who are in the place of God, that is, parents and the government. For it is proper for God and for everyone who is in a divine estate to be angry, to reprove and punish on account of those very persons who transgress this and the other commandments.

But the cause and need of this commandment is that God well knows that the world is evil, and that this life has much unhappiness; therefore, he has placed this and the other commandments between the good and the evil. Now, as there are many assaults upon all commandments, so it happens also in this commandment that we must live among many people who do us harm, so that we have cause to be hostile to them.

This commandment's aim is that no one offend his neighbor on account of any evil deed, even though he fully deserves it. For where murder is forbidden, all cause also is forbidden from which murder may originate. For many a one, although he does not kill, yet curses and utters a wish that would stop a person from running far if it were to strike him in the neck. Since this propensity resides in everyone by nature, and it is a common practice that no one is willing to suffer at the hands of another, God wishes to remove the root and source by which the heart is embittered against our neighbor and to accustom us to keep in view this commandment, to contemplate ourselves in it as in a mirror, and with hearty confidence and invocation of his name to commit to him the wrong which we suffer. Thus we shall allow our enemies to rage and be angry, doing what they can, while we learn to calm our wrath and to have a patient, gentle heart, especially toward those who give us cause to be angry, that is, our enemies.

The entire sum of what it means not to kill is to be impressed most explicitly upon the simpleminded. First, that we harm no one with our hand or by deed. Then, that we do not employ our tongue to instigate or counsel thereto. Further, that we neither use nor assent to any kind of means whereby anyone may be injured. And finally, that the heart be not ill-disposed toward anyone, nor from anger and hatred wish him ill, so that body and soul may be innocent in regard to everyone, but especially to those who wish you evil or inflict such upon you. For to do evil to one who wishes and does you good is not human, but diabolical.

Secondly, under this commandment, not only is the one who does evil to his neighbor guilty, but he also who could do him good, prevent and resist evil, defend and save him, so that no bodily harm or hurt happen to him, and yet does not do it. If, therefore, you send away one that is naked when you could clothe him, you have caused him to freeze to death. If you see one suffer hunger and do not give him food, you have caused him to starve. So also, if you see anyone innocently sentenced to death or in like distress, and do not save him, although you know ways and means to do so, you have killed him. You have withheld your love from him and deprived him of the benefit whereby his life would have been saved.

Therefore, God also rightly calls all those murderers who do not afford counsel and help in distress and danger of body and life, and will pass a most terrible sentence upon them in the last day, as Christ himself has announced when he shall say, as recorded in Matthew 25:42ff.: I was an hungered, and ye gave me no meat; I was thirsty, and ye gave me no drink; I was a stranger, and ye took me not in; naked, and ye clothed me not; sick and in prison and ye visited me not.

What else is that but to reproach them as murderers and bloodhounds? For although you have not actually done all this, you have nevertheless, so far as you were concerned, suffered the person to pine and perish in misfortune.

It is just as if I saw someone navigating and laboring in deep water [and struggling against adverse winds] or one fallen into fire, and could extend to him the hand to pull him out and save him, and yet refused to do it. What else would I appear, even in the eyes of the world, than as a murderer and a criminal?

It is God's ultimate purpose that we allow harm to befall no man, but show him all good and love, especially toward those who are our enemies. For to do good to our friends is but an ordinary heathen virtue, as Christ says in Matthew 5:46. Here we have again the Word of God whereby he would encourage and urge us to true, noble, and sublime works, as gentleness, patience, love, and kindness to our enemies, and would ever remind us that he will help, assist, and protect us, in order that he may thus quench the desire of revenge in us.

—*The Fifth Commandment, The Large Catechism*

QUESTIONS TO CONSIDER

1. How might a person be guilty of "murder in the heart"?
2. How can you guard your heart against this sin?

A PRAYERFUL RESPONSE

Lord, I long to love others as you do. Amen.

DAY 36

Unto the Generations

THOUGHT FOR TODAY
Marriage is a picture of Christ and his bride—the church.

WISDOM FROM SCRIPTURE
You shall not commit adultery.

EXODUS 20:14, NRSV

The Lord God took the man and put him in the garden of Eden to till it and keep it.

And the Lord God commanded the man, "You may freely eat of every tree of the garden; but of the tree of the knowledge of good and evil you shall not eat, for in the day that you eat of it you shall die."

Then the Lord God said, "It is not good that the man should be alone; I will make him a helper as his partner."

So out of the ground the Lord God formed every animal of the field and every bird of the air, and brought them to the man to see what he would call them; and whatever the man called every living creature, that was its name.

The man gave names to all cattle, and to the birds of the air, and to every animal of the field; but for the man there was not found a helper as his partner.

So the Lord God caused a deep sleep to fall upon the man, and he slept; then he took one of his ribs and closed up its place with flesh.

And the rib that the Lord God had taken from the man he

made into a woman and brought her to the man.

Then the man said,

"This at last is bone of my bones
and flesh of my flesh;
this one shall be called Woman,
for out of Man this one was taken."

Therefore a man leaves his father and his mother and clings
to his wife, and they become one flesh.

And the man and his wife were both naked, and were not
ashamed.

GENESIS 2:15-25, NRSV

INSIGHTS FROM MARTIN LUTHER

Since this commandment is aimed directly at the state of matrimony and gives occasion to speak of the same, you must well understand and mark first how gloriously God honors and extols this estate, inasmuch as by his commandment he both sanctions and guards it. He has hedged it about and protected it. Therefore he also wishes us to honor it and to maintain and conduct it as a divine and blessed estate; because he has instituted it before all others and therefore created man and woman separately, not for lewdness, but that they should [legitimately] live together, be fruitful, beget children, and nourish and train them to the honor of God.

Therefore, God has also most richly blessed this estate above all others, and, in addition, has bestowed on it and wrapped up in it everything in the world, to the end that this estate might be well and richly provided for. Married life is therefore no jest or presumption; but it is an excellent thing and a matter of divine seriousness. For it is of the highest importance to God that persons be raised who may serve the world and promote the knowledge of God, godly living, and all virtues, to fight against wickedness and the devil.

Therefore, I have always taught that this estate should not be despised nor held in disrepute, as is done by the blind world, but that it be regarded according to God's Word, by which it is adorned and sanctified, so that it is not only placed on an equality with other estates, but that it precedes and surpasses them all, whether they be that of emperor, princes, bishops, or whoever they please. For both ecclesiastical and civil estates must humble themselves and all be found in this estate as we shall hear. Therefore, it is not a peculiar estate, but the most common and noblest estate, which pervades all Christendom, yea which extends through all the world.

In the second place, you must know also that it is not only an honorable, but also a necessary state, and it is solemnly commanded by God that, in general, in all conditions, men and women, who were created for it, shall be found in this estate; yet with some exceptions (although few) whom God has especially excepted, so that they are not fit for the married estate, or whom he has released by a high, supernatural gift that they can maintain chastity without this estate. For where nature has its course, as it is implanted by God, it is not possible to remain chaste without marriage. For flesh and blood remain flesh and blood, and the natural inclination and excitement have their course without restraint or hindrance, as everybody sees and feels. In order that it may be the more easy in some degree to avoid unchastity, God has commanded the estate of matrimony, that everyone may have his proper portion and be satisfied therewith; although God's grace besides is required in order that the heart also may be pure.

Now, I speak of this in order that the young may be so guided that they conceive a liking for the married estate and know that it is a blessed estate and pleasing to God. For in this way we might in the course of time bring it about that married life be restored to honor, and that there might be less of the filthy, dissolute, disorderly doings which now run riot the world over in open prostitution and other shameful vices arising from disregard of married life. It is the duty of parents and the government to see to it that our youth be brought up to discipline and respectability, and when they have come to years of maturity, to provide for them [to have them married] in the fear of God and honorably.

Let me now say in conclusion that this commandment demands not only that everyone live chastely in thought, word, and deed in his condition, that is, especially in the estate of matrimony, but also that everyone love and esteem the spouse given him by God. For where conjugal chastity is to be maintained, man and wife must by all means live together in love and harmony, that one may cherish the other from the heart and with entire fidelity. For that is one of the principal points that kindle love and desire of chastity, so that, where this is found, chastity will follow as a matter of course without any command.

—*The Sixth Commandment, The Large Catechism*

QUESTIONS TO CONSIDER

1. If you are married, how can you strengthen that relationship?
2. Why is marriage sacred to God?

A PRAYERFUL RESPONSE

Lord, I pray for strength for the marriages of those I know. Amen.

DAY 37

The Common Vice

THOUGHT FOR TODAY

We can steal more than possessions.

WISDOM FROM SCRIPTURE

You shall not steal.

EXODUS 20:15, NRSV

You shall not have in your bag two kinds of weights, large and small.

You shall not have in your house two kinds of measures, large and small.

You shall have only a full and honest weight; you shall have only a full and honest measure, so that your days may be long in the land that the Lord your God is giving you.

For all who do such things, all who act dishonestly, are abhorrent to the Lord your God.

DEUTERONOMY 25:13-16, NRSV

When someone steals an ox or a sheep, and slaughters it or sells it, the thief shall pay five oxen for an ox, and four sheep for a sheep. The thief shall make restitution, but if unable to do so, shall be sold for the theft.

EXODUS 22:1-3, NRSV

Thou shalt not steal.

To steal is to signify not only to empty our neighbor's coffer and pockets, but to be grasping in the market, in all stores, booths, wine and beer cellars, workshops, and, in short, wherever there is trading or taking and giving of money for merchandise or labor.

When a manservant or maidservant does not serve faithfully in the house, and does damage, or allows it to be done when it could be prevented, or otherwise ruins and neglects the goods entrusted to him, from indolence, idleness, or malice, and in whatever way this can be done purposely (for I do not speak of what happens from oversight and against one's will), you can in a year abscond thirty or forty florins, which if another had taken secretly or carried away, he would be hanged with the rope. But here you [while conscious of such a great theft] may even bid defiance and become insolent, and no one dare call you a thief.

The same I say also of mechanics, workmen, and day laborers, who all follow their wanton notions, and never know enough ways to overcharge people, while they are lazy and unfaithful in their work. All these are far worse than sneak-thieves, against whom we can guard with locks and bolts, or who, if apprehended, are treated in such a manner that they will not do the same again. But against these no one can guard, no one dare even look awry at them or accuse them of theft, so that one would ten times rather lose from his purse. For here are my neighbors, good friends, my own servants, from whom I expect good [every faithful and diligent service], who defraud me first of all.

Furthermore, in the market and in common trade likewise, this practice is in full swing, where one openly defrauds another with bad merchandise, false measures, weights, coins, and by nimbleness and queer finances or dexterous tricks takes advantage of him; likewise, when one overcharges a person in a trade and wantonly drives a hard bargain, he skins and distresses him. And who can recount or think of all these things? To sum up, this is the commonest craft and the largest guild on earth, and if we regard the world throughout all conditions of life, it is nothing else than a vast, wide stall full of great thieves.

This is, in short, the course of the world: Whoever can steal and rob openly goes free and secure, unmolested by anyone, and even demands that he be honored. Meanwhile, the little sneak thieves who have once trespassed must bear the shame and punishment to render the former godly and honorable. But let them know that in the sight of God they are the greatest thieves, and that he will punish them as they are worthy and deserve.

Such shall be the lot also of mechanics and day laborers of whom we are now obliged to hear and suffer such intolerable maliciousness, as though they were noblemen in another's possessions, and everyone were obliged to give them what they demand. Just let them continue practicing their exactions as long as they can; but God will not forget his commandment, and will reward them according as they have served, and will hang them, not upon a green gallows, but upon a dry one so that all their life they shall neither prosper nor accumulate anything. And indeed, if there were a well-ordered government in the land, such wantonness might soon be checked and prevented, as was the custom in ancient times among the Romans, where such characters were promptly seized by the pate in a way that others took warning.

No more shall all the rest prosper who change the open free market into a carrion-pit of extortion and a den of robbery, where the poor are daily overcharged, new burdens and high prices are imposed, and everyone uses the market according to his caprice and is even defiant and brags as though it were his fair privilege and right to sell his goods for as high a price as he please, and no one had a right to say a word against it. We will indeed look on and let these people skin, pinch, and hoard, but we will trust in God that, after you have been skinning and scraping for a long time, he will pronounce such a blessing on your gains that your grain in the garner, your beer in the cellar, your cattle in the stalls shall perish; yea, where you have cheated and overcharged anyone to the amount of a florin, your entire pile shall be consumed with rust, so that you shall never enjoy it.

And indeed, we see and experience this being fulfilled daily before our eyes, that no stolen or dishonestly acquired possession thrives. How many there are who rake and scrape day and night and yet grow not a farthing richer! And though they gather much, they must suffer so many plagues and misfortunes that they cannot relish it with cheerfulness nor transmit it to their children.

In short, if you steal much, depend upon it that again as much will be stolen from you; and he who robs and acquires with violence and wrong will submit to one who shall deal after the same fashion with him. For God is master of this art, that since everyone robs and steals from the other, he punishes one thief by means of another. Else where should we find enough gallows and ropes?

Now, whoever is willing to be instructed let him know that this is the commandment of God, and that it must not be treated as a jest. For although you despise us, defraud, steal, and rob, we will indeed manage to endure your haughtiness, suffer, and, according to the Lord's Prayer, forgive and show pity; for we know that the godly shall nevertheless have enough, and you injure yourself more than another.

We have exhorted, warned, and protested enough; he who will not heed or believe it may go on until he learns this by experience. Yet it must be impressed upon the young that they may be careful not to follow the old lawless crowd, but keep their eyes fixed upon God's commandment, lest his wrath and punishment come upon them too.

—*The Seventh Commandment, The Large Catechism*

QUESTIONS TO CONSIDER

1. In what ways could a person steal from God?
2. Is stealing ever a temptation to you? Why or why not?

A PRAYERFUL RESPONSE

Lord, reveal in me any area where I might be stealing from you or others. Amen.

DAY 38

Loving Your Neighbor

THOUGHT FOR TODAY
It is easier to destroy a reputation than to rebuild one.

WISDOM FROM SCRIPTURE
You shall not bear false witness against your neighbor.

EXODUS 20:16, NRSV

O Lord, who may abide in your tent?
Who may dwell on your holy hill?
Those who walk blamelessly,
and do what is right,
and speak the truth from their heart;
who do not slander with their tongue,
and do no evil to their friends,
nor take up a reproach against their neighbors;
in whose eyes the wicked are despised,
but who honor those who fear the Lord;
who stand by their oath even to their hurt;
who do not lend money at interest,
and do not take a bribe against the innocent.
Those who do these things shall never be moved.

PSALM 15:1-5, NRSV

INSIGHTS FROM MARTIN LUTHER
It is intolerable to live among men in open shame and general
contempt. Therefore, God wishes the reputation, good name,

and upright character of our neighbor to be taken away or diminished as little as his money and possessions, that everyone may stand in his integrity before wife, children, servants, and neighbors. And in the first place, we take the plainest meaning of this commandment according to the words [Thou shalt not bear false witness], as pertaining to the public courts of justice, where a poor, innocent man is accused and oppressed by false witnesses in order to be punished in his body, property, or honor.

This commandment is given first of all that everyone shall help his neighbor to secure his rights, and not allow them to be hindered or twisted, but shall promote and strictly maintain them. And especially is a goal set up here for our jurists that they be careful to deal truly and uprightly with every case, allowing right to remain right, and not perverting anything [by their tricks and technical points turning black into white and making wrong out to be right], nor glossing it over or keeping silent concerning it, irrespective of a person's money, possession, honor, or power. This is one part and the plainest sense of this commandment concerning all that takes place in court.

This commandment forbids all sins of the tongue whereby we may injure or approach too closely to our neighbor. For to bear false witness is nothing else than a work of the tongue. Now, whatever is done with the tongue against a fellowman God would have prohibited, whether it be false preachers with their doctrine and blasphemy, false judges and witnesses with their verdict, or outside of court by lying and evil-speaking. Here belongs particularly the detestable, shameful vice of speaking behind a person's back and slandering, to which the devil spurs us on. For it is a common evil plague that everyone prefers hearing evil to hearing good of his neighbor; and although we ourselves are so bad that we cannot suffer that anyone should say anything bad about us, yet we cannot bear that the best is spoken about others.

Those, then, are called slanderers who are not content with knowing a thing, but proceed to assume jurisdiction, and when they know a slight offense of another, carry it into every corner and are delighted and tickled that they can stir up another's displeasure [baseness], as swine roll themselves in the dirt and root in it with the snout. This is nothing else than meddling with the judgment and office of God, and pronouncing sentence and punishment with the most severe verdict. For no judge can punish to a higher degree nor go farther than to say: "He is a thief, a murderer, a traitor," etc. Therefore, whoever presumes to say the same of his neighbor goes just as far as the emperor and all governments. For although you do not wield the sword, you employ your poisonous tongue to the shame and hurt of your neighbor.

God, therefore, would have it prohibited that anyone speak evil of another, even though he be guilty and the latter know it right well; much less if he do not know it and have it only from hearsay. But you say: Shall I not say it if it be the truth? Answer: Why do you not make accusation to regular judges? Ah, I cannot prove it publicly, and hence I might be silenced and turned away in a harsh manner [incur the penalty of a false accusation]. "Ah, indeed, do you smell the roast?" If you do not trust yourself to stand before the proper authorities and to make answer, then hold your tongue. But if you know it, know it for yourself and not for another. For if you tell it to others, although it

188

be true, you will appear as a liar, because you cannot prove it, and besides you are acting like a knave. For we ought never to deprive anyone of his honor or good name unless it be first taken away from him publicly.

False witness, then, is everything which cannot be properly proved. Therefore, what is not manifest upon sufficient evidence no one shall make public or declare for truth. In short, whatever is secret should be allowed to remain secret, or should be secretly reproved. Therefore, if you encounter an idle tongue that betrays and slanders someone, contradict such a one promptly to his face, that he may blush. Thus many a one will hold his tongue who otherwise would bring some poor man into bad repute from which he would not easily extricate himself. For honor and a good name are easily taken away but not easily restored.

—*The Eighth Commandment, The Large Catechism*

QUESTIONS TO CONSIDER

1. How do you recognize when you are speaking falsely about someone?
2. Why are we so prone to listen for negatives rather than positives about others?

A PRAYERFUL RESPONSE

Lord, help me to speak truthfully and with integrity. Amen.

DAY 39

No Need to Covet

THOUGHT FOR TODAY

If we covet what is not ours, we sin.

WISDOM FROM SCRIPTURE

You shall not covet your neighbor's house; you shall not covet your neighbor's wife, or male or female slave, or ox, or donkey, or anything that belongs to your neighbor.

EXODUS 20:17, NRSV

But the thing that David had done displeased the Lord, and the Lord sent Nathan to David. He came to him, and said to him, "There were two men in a certain city, the one rich and the other poor.

"The rich man had very many flocks and herds;

"But the poor man had nothing but one little ewe lamb, which he had bought. He brought it up, and it grew up with him and with his children; it used to eat of his meager fare, and drink from his cup, and lie in his bosom, and it was like a daughter to him.

"Now there came a traveler to the rich man, and he was loath to take one of his own flock or herd to prepare for the wayfarer who had come to him, but he took the poor man's lamb, and prepared that for the guest who had come to him."

Then David's anger was greatly kindled against the man. He said to Nathan, "As the Lord lives, the man who has done this deserves to die; he shall restore the lamb fourfold, because he did this thing, and because he had no pity."

Nathan said to David, "You are the man! Thus says the Lord, the God of Israel: I anointed you king over Israel, and I rescued you from the hand of Saul;

"I gave you your master's house, and your master's wives into your bosom, and gave you the house of Israel and of Judah; and if that had been too little, I would have added as much more.

"Why have you despised the word of the Lord, to do what is evil in his sight?"

2 SAMUEL 12:1-9, NRSV

INSIGHTS FROM MARTIN LUTHER

Thou shalt not covet thy neighbor's house. Thou shalt not covet thy neighbor's wife, nor his manservant, nor his maidservant, nor his cattle, nor anything that is his.

These two commandments are given quite exclusively to the Jews; nevertheless, in part they also concern us. For they do not interpret them as referring to unchastity or theft, because these are sufficiently forbidden in Scripture. They also thought that they had kept all those when they had done or not done the external act. Therefore, God has added these two commandments in order that it be esteemed as sin and forbidden to desire or in any way to aim at getting our neighbor's wife or possessions; and especially because under the Jewish government menservants and maidservants were not free as now to serve for wages as long as they pleased, but were their master's property with their body and all they had, as cattle and other possessions.

Moreover, every man had power over his wife to put her

away publicly by giving her a bill of divorce, and to take another. Therefore, they were in constant danger among each other that if one took a fancy to another's wife, he might allege any reason both to dismiss his own wife and to estrange the other's wife from him, that he might obtain her under pretext of right. That was not considered a sin or disgrace with them; as little as now with hired help, when a proprietor dismisses his manservant or maidservant, or takes another's servants from him in any way.

For we are so inclined by nature that no one desires to see another have as much as himself, and each one acquires as much as he can; the other may fare as best he can. And yet we pretend to be godly, know how to adorn ourselves most finely and conceal our rascality, resort to and invent adroit devices and deceitful artifices (such as now are daily most ingeniously contrived) as though they were derived from the law codes; yea, we even dare impertinently to refer to it, and boast of it, and will not have it called rascality, but shrewdness and caution. In this lawyers and jurists assist, who twist and stretch the law to suit it to their cause, stress words and use them for a subterfuge, irrespective of equity or their neighbor's necessity. And, in short, whoever is the most expert and cunning in these affairs finds most help in law, as they themselves say: *Vigilantibus iura subveniunt* [that is, the laws favor the watchful].

This last commandment therefore is given not for rogues in the eyes of the world, but for the most pious, who wish to be praised and be called honest and upright people, since they have not offended against the former commandments, as especially the Jews claimed to be, and even now many great noblemen, gentlemen, and princes. For the other common masses belong yet farther down, under the Seventh Commandment, as those who are not much concerned whether they acquire their possessions with honor and right.

Now, this occurs most frequently in cases that are brought into court, where it is the purpose to get something from our neighbor and to force him out of his own. For example, when people quarrel and wrangle about a large inheritance or real estate, they avail themselves of, and resort to, whatever has the appearance of right, so dressing and adorning everything that the law must favor their side, and they keep the property with such title that no one can make complaint or lay claim to it.

In whatever way such things happen, we must know that God does not wish that you deprive your neighbor of anything that belongs to him so that he suffer the loss and you gratify your avarice with it, even if you could keep it honorably before the world; for it is a secret and insidious imposition practiced under the hat, as we say, that it may not be observed. For although you go your way as if you had done no one any wrong, you have nevertheless injured your neighbor; and if it is not called stealing and cheating, yet it is called coveting your neighbor's property, that is, aiming at possession of it, enticing it away from him without his will, and being unwilling to see him enjoy what God has granted him.

Therefore, we allow these commandments to remain in their ordinary meaning, that it is commanded, first, that we do not desire our neighbor's damage, nor even assist nor give occasion for it, but gladly wish and leave him what he has, and, besides, advance and preserve for him what may be for his profit and service, as we should wish to be treated. Thus these commandments are especially directed against envy and miserable avarice, God wishing to remove all causes and sources whence arises everything by which we do injury to our neighbor, and therefore he expresses it in plain words: Thou shalt not covet. For he would especially have the heart pure, although we shall never attain to that as long as we live here; so that this commandment will remain, like all the rest, one that will constantly accuse us and show how ungodly we are in the sight of God!

—*The Ninth and Tenth Commandments,*
The Large Catechism

QUESTIONS TO CONSIDER

1. What are you tempted to covet?
2. How can you ask God to meet that need?

A PRAYERFUL RESPONSE

Lord, may I receive what I need from you alone. Amen.

Respecting the Commands

THOUGHT FOR TODAY

God's laws are good.

WISDOM FROM SCRIPTURE

Happy are those whose way is blameless,
who walk in the law of the Lord.
Happy are those who keep his decrees,
who seek him with their whole heart,
who also do no wrong,
but walk in his ways.
You have commanded your precepts
to be kept diligently.
O that my ways may be steadfast
in keeping your statutes!
Then I shall not be put to shame,
having my eyes fixed on all your commandments.
I will praise you with an upright heart,
when I learn your righteous ordinances.
I will observe your statutes;
do not utterly forsake me.

How can young people keep their way pure?
By guarding it according to your word.
With my whole heart I seek you;
do not let me stray from your commandments.
I treasure your word in my heart,
so that I may not sin against you.
Blessed are you, O Lord;
teach me your statutes.

With my lips I declare
all the ordinances of your mouth.
I delight in the way of your decrees
as much as in all riches.
I will meditate on your precepts,
and fix my eyes on your ways.
I will delight in your statutes;
I will not forget your word.

PSALM 119:1-16, NRSV

INSIGHTS FROM MARTIN LUTHER

We have the Ten Commandments, a compendium of divine doctrine of what we are to do in order that our whole life may be pleasing to God. From them everything must arise and flow that is to be a good work, so that outside of the Ten Commandments no work or thing can be good or pleasing to God, however great or precious it be in the eyes of the world.

I am of the opinion that here one will find his hands full, [and will have enough] to do to observe these, namely, meekness, patience, and love towards enemies, chastity, kindness, etc., and what such virtues imply. But such works are not of value and make no display in the eyes of the world; for they are not peculiar and conceited works and restricted to particular times, places, rites, and customs, but are common, everyday domestic works which one neighbor can practice toward another; therefore they are not of high esteem.

All this I say and urge in order that men might become rid of the sad misuse which has taken such deep root and still cleaves to everybody, and in all estates upon earth become used to looking hither only, and to being concerned about these matters. For it will be a long time before they will produce a doctrine or estates equal to the Ten Commandments, because they are so high that no one can attain to them by human power; and whoever does attain to them is a heavenly, angelic man far above all holiness of the world. Only occupy yourself with them, and try your best, apply all power and ability, and you will find so much to do that you will neither seek nor esteem any other work or holiness.

From this it again appears how highly these Ten Commandments are to be exalted and extolled above all estates, commandments, and works which are taught and practiced aside from them. For here we can boast and say: Let all the wise and saints step forth and produce, if they can, a [single] work like these commandments, upon which God insists with such earnestness, and which he enjoins with his greatest wrath and punishment, and, besides, adds such glorious promises that he will pour out upon us all good things and blessings. Therefore, they should be taught above all others, and be esteemed precious and dear as the highest treasure given by God.

—*Conclusion of the Ten Commandments,*
The Large Catechism

QUESTIONS TO CONSIDER
1. Which commandment most challenges you?
2. How does grace relate to the Ten Commandments?

A PRAYERFUL RESPONSE
Lord, teach me to love and obey your laws. Amen.

WORKS BY MARTIN LUTHER

Some of the many works of Martin Luther can be found at the following Internet address:

http://www.ic/net.org/pub/resources/text/wittenberg-luther.html

ABOUT THE COMPILERS

With the *Life Messages* devotional series, **Judith Couchman** hopes you'll be encouraged and enlightened by people who have shared their spiritual journeys through the printed word.

Judith owns Judith & Company, a writing and editing business. She has also served as the creator and founding editor-in-chief of *Clarity* magazine, managing editor of *Christian Life,* editor of *Sunday Digest,* director of communications for The Navigators, and director of new product development for NavPress.

Besides speaking to women's and professional groups, Judith is the author or compiler of thirty-nine books and many magazine articles. In addition, she has received numerous awards for her work in secondary education, religious publishing, and corporate communications.

Lisa Marzano is Director of Special Projects for International Students Inc., and a freelance writer. She spends much of her time organizing large conferences and events, and trying to find more time to write.

Both compilers live in Colorado.